Interventions is produced on the land of the Wurundjeri people of the Kulin Nation. We acknowledge the Traditional Owners of country throughout Australia and recognise their continuing connection to land, waters and culture. We pay our respects to their Elders past, present and emerging. Their land was stolen, never ceded.

It always was and always will be Aboriginal land.

This manuscript was completed with the assistance of a Varuna Writing Residency and the Key West Writers Workshop in the USA, and was largely written on Nugunnawal land.

A Darker Shade of Moonlite

A creative biography

First published 2023 by Interventions Inc

Interventions is a not-for-profit, independent, radical book publisher. For further information:
www.interventions.org.au
info@interventions.org.au
PO Box 963, Coffs Harbour,
NSW, Australia, 2450

Queer Oz Folk Series Vol 3
Series editor: Graham Willett
Queer Oz Folk publishes Australian queer history in good quality, affordable editions with an eye to the widest possible audiences.
www.queer.oz.folk

Cover design and layout by Simon Strong
Interior design and layout by Viktoria Ivanova
Front over photo: Young men bathing in bush creek, W. H. Smith, [ca. 1885-ca. 1899], State Library of Victoria, is004268

Author: Craig Cormick

Title: A Darker Shade of Moonlite: A Creative Biography
ISBN: 978-0-6452534-8-1 Paperback
ISBN: 978-0-6452534-9-8 e-book

© Craig Cormick 2023

The moral rights of the author have been asserted.
All rights reserved. Except as permitted under the Australian Copyright Act 1968 (for example, a fair dealing for the purposes of study, research, criticism or review), no part of this book may be reproduced, stored in a retrieval system, communicated or transmitted in any form or by any means without prior written permission.

All inquiries should be made to the author.

 A catalogue record for this book is available from the National Library of Australia

The one duty we owe to history is to rewrite it.

– Oscar Wilde

This book is entirely true – except for all the bits that aren't.

Andrew George Scott, alias Captain Moonlite (State Library of Victoria)

He called himself Captain Moonlite!

He called himself Captain Moonlite, like he was some kind of superhero, and I suppose to us boys he was. If you look him up in books on bushrangers – if you find him there at all – he'll only have a short entry, which will probably describe him as 'one of the most curious', or 'most charismatic' or 'possessed of a split personality'. He was all of those to us too.

It would piss him off, though, to see how little a piece of history he's been left with. We were going to be the last great bushranger gang. We were going to be bigger than the Kellys. And that was something that really wound him up. The bloody Kellys! If they'd just let the police shoot the shit out of them in the Wombat Ranges, or retired to the Gold Coast like any decent criminal, we'd have endless books and TV documentaries made of us instead. Family station wagons loaded with kids and their Kmart crap would detour off the Hume Highway, to drive to Wagga Wagga to visit the Moonlite theme park to see the robots and holograms of us re-enacting our final shoot-out.

But the Kelly gang went out in a big bang, with bloody metal helmets and armour, as if a film producer had advised them on the strong visual appeal of it. Who could resist that? Of course they stole our publicity. And they did it right next to the bloody Hume Highway too. How could they not be the poster boys of bushranger tourism?

But I'm getting ahead of myself. Here we were, setting off from Melbourne in the Spring of 1879. Five young lads and our mentor (or tormentor) Moonlite, convinced we were trekking towards our fame and fortune, arguing over who would play us in the movies they'd be making – not knowing that young Gus Wernicke, only 15 years old, was just days away from being shot dead at that terrible shoot-out with the police near Wantabadgery station. James Nesbitt was going to die too. Moonlite's favourite. And that's when it all fell apart. Moonlite probably could have shot his way out of the police circle and escaped, but the fight suddenly went out of him. As though Nesbitt was the foundation upon which he'd constructed his delusion. Not that he had any shortage of delusions – but we'll get to those by and by.

- - -

One of the problems with writing your own history

You may have heard it said that one of the problems with writing your own history is that other people are busy writing their own versions of it as well. And yes, there are some elements of truth among all those things you can read about Moonlite, but I'll tell you two truths that anybody who has ended up in the cross-hairs of any historian or random writer's target sights won't dispute. Firstly, most people's histories are as much about themselves as the character they are writing about; secondly, Moonlite was too complex for any single person to capture him accurately.

I've been asked many times to describe how I first met Moonlite, and I generally tell it like this: 'It is unknown how and when young Graham Bennett first came under Moonlite's fateful influence.' I like the idea of keeping people guessing. Some historians claim that I, like most of the other boys, met him at one of his lectures on prison reform around Melbourne. Others claim that he collected me near Albury, where I was living destitute. Others say that I was hitching a ride along the Hume Highway when I fell in with the gang.

After the shoot-out at Wantabadgery, it's on the record that I was wounded in the arm and taken to Gundagai for the initial hearing and then on to Sydney for the trial. I was found guilty and sentenced to be hanged, like Moonlite and Thomas Rogan, but my sentence was commuted to life imprisonment. You might hear a rumour that I was hanged there for attempted murder of another inmate. But the truth of it is, I just slipped quietly out of the pages of history.

The historians have managed to dig up a few facts about me, though. I was an English sailor, born in Yorkshire or Wessex. I came to Australia aboard the ship *Himalaya* or the *Georgette*, in 1877 or earlier – although neither ship is recorded as coming to Australia. I jumped ship in Melbourne, or perhaps Adelaide. I was tempted by the promise of easy wealth on the goldfields. I was running away. I was looking for adventure. I was just having a gap year.

You get the picture? No wonder the historians have tended to concentrate on the other four lads in the gang – young Gus Wernicke, Thomas Rogan, Thomas Williams and, of course, James Nesbitt, Moonlite's 'chum'. None of us over 21 years of age.

But you really need to understand Moonlite to understand us. What was it about him that drew us into his embrace? Well, that's complex too. He had a presence that we'd never encountered before. He was tall, with a handsomely groomed full beard and dark hair, but you really remembered his piercing blue eyes. And when he talked to you, you felt you were the only one in the room who mattered. That meant a lot to us young lads – who were largely on our own, kicked around and ignored by society. He was somebody. He was educated. He had travelled widely. Mixed in high society (before serving time in prison). And he was interested in us. It was a wonderful feeling to be in his company. And he probably thought it pretty good to have us lads admiring him the way we did, too, because he loved an audience. We were like oxygen for his ego. So each fed off the other, creating a strong and binding relationship.

If he'd been a teacher or a youth worker, he'd have been praised as a great social role model. You'd see stories about him in the Saturday magazine sections of the newspapers. Sitting at your café, sipping lattes or cappuccinos, you'd read that he took five boys into the bush and toughened them up, made them independent and self-assured, and all that guff. But he was a criminal, so he was condemned as a bad influence, preying on us boys for his own ends.

It still mightn't have ended up so badly, I sometimes think, if he was more stable. But that's one of the problems about being close to somebody unstable – you really only see it clearly in retrospect.

Sorry – I'm starting to sound like a bloody historian!

- - -

Sneaking out of Melbourne

So here we were, sneaking out of Melbourne, led on by Moonlite's stories of how the police were gunning for us. We'd have freedom, he promised us, if we could just escape their tyranny. It was true enough that there didn't seem much future for any of us in Melbourne. Times were hard, and it wasn't easy for a notorious bushranger to get a job, earn an income and be treated with the respect that Moonlite felt was due to him from society.

I think that's one of the reasons he recruited us boys around him. He'd been used to hobnobbing in high society and, now that he was shunned, he needed something to replace it. He needed adulation. He needed his groupies – and that was us. Well, except for James Nesbitt, of course. He was the number one boy. Reporters at the time described him as Moonlite's 'chum', or 'companion', like it was a special code that everyone at the time would read, then nod their head and lay one finger alongside their nose and mumble, 'wink, wink, nod, nod, say no more!'

I wonder whether the euphemisms ever meant anything deeper to anyone other than the writers who used them, though. A strange bloody lot, writers. They expect every reader to get the same meaning out of what they wrote as they intended. To quote a great Australian philosopher, 'They're dreaming!'

Anyhoo – we soon discovered that times were even harder out in rural-and-regional Australia. Take into account a drought, a recession, labour market imbalances and structural adjustments, and we were too big a group to be easily offered itinerant labour. The country was full of blokes wandering around, in ones or twos, knocking on farm house doors and asking for a bit of work in exchange for a meal. Most places would have something one or two men could do, like chop some wood or clear some brush – but we were half a bloody cricket team, and that was a more difficult proposition altogether.

So we trod the dirt roads, carrying our possessions on our backs, heading north to the promised land. And the tougher things got, the better Moonlite's stories about our future got. He had a property up in New South Wales, and he just had to sort out some legal issues, and then we'd be able to move onto it and live in freedom from harassment. Or we were going to take a ship to Fiji, where a white man could live like a king. The weather was warm, and the people were kind, and exotic sweet fruits grew on trees all around.

He'd sit there beside our meagre fire at nights and tell us of his visits to Fiji and what a land it was. There were no police. The land was rich and the natives welcoming, and anybody willing to put in half a day's work could be running a successful plantation in no time.

'What will we grow?' we asked him.

'Whatever we like,' he said. 'The land there is so fertile that if you poke a walking stick into the soil in the morning, you'll find shoots growing on the end of it by sunset.'

'I've heard the natives are cannibals there?' we might ask.

'They are afraid of firearms,' he'd say, brandishing his gun. He insisted that we all learn how to use guns. He said it was vital – for Fiji, of course. He'd have us all armed with the best pistols, rifles and shotguns we could obtain, he said, even though most of the pieces we now had were old and worn, probably as much a danger to us as the target.

'You're powerful when you have a gun,' he said, 'and you don't even need to shoot anyone to have that power. The fear of a gun is a very powerful thing to wield over any man, civilised or savage.' So we'd wave the pistols around as if we were powerful men. Like we were a fierce gang of bushrangers rather than playing cowboys.

We lapped it all up, of course, like the young mugs that we were. We could almost see it there before us. We'd sail in like Captain Cook arriving in Tahiti, and the native women and men would swim out to the ship, naked, and climb aboard and press necklaces of flowers and shells onto us. We'd spend our days swinging in hammocks by the sea, watching our fortunes grow around us. Coffee, apples, potatoes, wheat, pineapples, limes, bananas and things we couldn't even pronounce properly – like – cumquats, persimmons or pomegranates, guarana and loquats. We'd dream what they might taste like, imagining each fruit's sticky juice as we lay down to sleep under our thin blankets, footsore and hungry with nothing but brown creek water to quench our thirst.

It kept us walking though. If we faltered, he would shift the dream to a closer

Moonlite's 'chum' James Nesbitt, woodcut by Alfred May and Alfred Martin Ebsworth (SLV)

one. The property in New South Wales, which wasn't so far away. During the daytime, when the exotic dreams had faded, that was something not too unimaginable to reach. Just a few more days' walking, always just a few more. We'd be able to rest up there. Have a good feed. Spend a bit of time earning some money and deciding what we wanted to do.

He had this way of spending some time alone with you on the walk. Just you and him talking, and he'd look at you with those piercing blue eyes of his and smile and nod his head, just so, and he'd make you feel absolutely vital to the plan. The most important one of all the boys – except for Nesbitt, of course. And that was such a wonderful feeling! Like the intoxicating taste of exotic fruits to a person who'd only ever dreamed of them. You'd keep following him for miles and miles just to taste a little more of that.

- - -

In the movie, we'd cut to the back story

This is the place in the movie where we'd cut to a bit of the back story, so I'll tell you the types of things you could learn from Wikipedia if you bothered to look them up. Captain Moonlite was born in Ireland and is a Kilkenny-based underground Irish rapper who lists his influences as Guinness, Hurling, Crass and Adam and the Ants. Sorry, wrong Captain Moonlite, but it just goes to show you how strong an influence he's had.

Our bloke was possibly born in Ireland in 1845, or perhaps 1842, and was baptised Andrew George Scott in the village of Rathfriland in County Down, north of Belfast in Northern Ireland. His father was an Anglican clergyman of Scottish descent, described as having a fascination with engineering. Some historians, or pretend authors, credit him with constructing a massive waterworks around their garden.

The *Town and Country Journal* published a major profile of Moonlite on 29 November 1879, before he was hanged, saying:

> His father originally intended the boy to study for the church, but finding that he was of a too lively disposition he allowed him to choose his own calling.

He chose the navy and did a stint as a cadet on board the *H.M.S. Britannia*. He then trained as an engineer, finishing his studies in London just in time to join the family as they migrated to New Zealand in 1861.

At this point, things become a little bit confusing, and you could choose to believe any of several different stories. One story relates a scandalous affair with a young married woman named Zoe Kirtle, which saw him sent abroad. According to another story, he took himself off to the continent while studying engineering, supposedly to inspect the Roman aqueducts – but he ended up joining the army of the Italian revolutionary Giuseppe Garibaldi, in 1860, helping him to unite Italy into a single dysfunctional nation. Garibaldi's men were called the red shirts – because they wore red shirts, of course, designed to hide the blood if a man was wounded and not to fill his comrades with fear. In World War I, the British army, learning from this, moved from white trousers to brown or khaki.

The story goes that Scott took part in several campaigns, including Garibaldi's march on Naples, despite speaking no Italian. He was wounded in the shoulder and returned to England in late 1860.

Back in England, he fell in with dubious friends and became convinced that a young man with a head for adventure should try his luck on the goldfields of Victoria or New Zealand. This enticed him to seek passage as an engineer on board the *Black Eagle*. He arrived alone in New Zealand in 1861.

Another story is that his father, Thomas Scott, travelled to New Zealand in 1861 to take up a position as minister, taking the whole family with him. Young Andrew ended up on the goldfields of Otago, hoping to make his fortune, as a young man in a new country might be wont to do. If his parents had known the path he would be taking from there, though, they might rather have chosen the poverty of rural Ireland for the family. We'll never know, of course. We could make up their thoughts, admittedly, but how can you trust an author who makes up people's thoughts?

Here the paths of the story diverge yet again. He discovered that gold was not so easy to find as stories had suggested, and the Māori wars were making times difficult for a lone man seeking his fortune. So he joined a local militia – the 700th Regiment or the Waikato volunteers or the Auckland Volunteer Engineers Corps. He was involved in some capacity in the battle for Waikato and wounded in both legs by bullets or spears or clubs or perhaps shot by his own men, if you want to add that to the list. He was brought back to Auckland or somewhere to convalesce and spent many months in hospital recovering. Far too many months, it seems, for he was accused of malingering, to which he responded that taking part in killing women and children was not war. He had no stomach, heart or liver for such wars and would rather lie in hospital chatting up nurses and orderlies all day long. As a result, he was dishonourably discharged, or perhaps court martialled, from the army or the militia or the volunteers – or not.

He next decided to try his fortunes on the goldfields of California, travelling

No. 2170   Name A. G. Scott als Capt" Moonlight

Date when Portrait was taken 26th Nov' 1879

8269.79

Native place	Ireland
Year of birth	1843
Arrived in Colony — Ship	Eken Allen
Year	1867
Trade or occupation previous to conviction	Civil Engineer
Religion	C of E
Education, degree of	R & W
Height	5 feet 9¼ inches
Weight in lbs. On committal	143
On discharge	
Colour of hair	Brown
Colour of eyes	Grey
Marks or special features	—

Where and when tried: Sup. Ct Court 11 Dec. 79
Offence: Murder
Sentence: Death
Remarks: —

Executed 20 Jany 1880

(No. of previous Portrait)

PREVIOUS CONVICTIONS.

Where and When.			Offence.	Sentence.	
Sy Qr Ses.	Dec. 20	70	False pretences	12 months L.	Concurrent
Do.	" 21		Do.	18 do L.	
Ballarat Genl Ses.		1872	Bank robbery under Arms	10 Years Roads	

to the USA sometime around 1864. Once there, he ended up, inexplicably, on the eastern side of the country and joined the Union army, under General Grant, or Sherman, working under the quartermaster, or taking part in campaigns such as the battles of Skimming and Blackmarketing – and we might as well throw in Gettysburg for good measure, even though it was the previous year. Done with the fighting and sporting a few more battle wounds, he somehow left the army, or was dismissed, or woke up from the dream of it and then appeared in California again, where he fell in with a conman named Archie Telford.

Together, they travelled to Australia via the Pacific island of Fiji, where he took part in some ventures involving acquiring land, because he had dreams of establishing a plantation growing something. He then went to New Caledonia and, from there, ended up travelling to Sydney.

It may be that he was lured to Sin-City by the goldfields in New South Wales. It may be that he was simply accompanying Archie Telford on a job. Or he may have been involved in smuggling escaped prisoners out of the French prison on New Caledonia. Or not.

Once he arrives in Sydney, though, the stories start to converge a little more. But just a little. Being the son of a clergyman, well-educated and convinced of his own self-importance, Andrew George Scott wasted no time in introducing himself to select members of Sydney Society. He soon impressed the colonials and TV executives with his flair for chit-chat and charm. However his stay in New South Wales came to an enforced end when a woman he had been seeing regularly, known only as Evilin, or perhaps Emma, told him that she might be pregnant, or perhaps her husband was out of prison in New Caledonia, where he had been arrested for trying to smuggle out a French prisoner. Or not. He then told her that he had to return to Ireland because his father, who was actually living in New Zealand, had taken ill. Or he was caught up in a scandal involving shares in resource companies with members of the right wing of the New South Wales Labor Party. Or he was photographed with a 'person of interest' at a 'house of ill-repute'. Take your pick, really.

Anyway, the outcome of it was that he ended up in Melbourne in the year of our Lord 1868, which is when the paths stop meandering around so much and converge into a more or less agreed story. He had an introduction to the Anglican Bishop of Melbourne, Charles Perry, who apparently took a liking to our lad. He appointed him a lay reader – or an L-plate minister – at the small town of Bacchus Marsh, about 60 kilometres from Melbourne, with the expectation being he would enter the Anglican priesthood upon completion of his service there.

Yeah, good luck with that Charlie!

- - -

He was a great favourite with some

We can push the fast forward button on things a little bit here, but the Reader's Digest condensed version is that he and the members of Bacchus Marsh high society really hit it off.

According to the biopic in the *Town and Country Journal*:

> He was a great favourite with some, though a few considered him a scamp and hypocrite, and many insisted that he was mad, and all the marvellous tales he was narrating of his prowess were pure inventions.

Things fell apart when he was drawn into a murky court case involving perjury, while acting as a witness for a friend accused of cattle stealing from a respectable, but unfortunately named, local family – the Crooks. But Victoria has always had its fair share of respectable Crooks, has it not? The church did what it has always been good at doing, and transferred him – not quite disgraced, but certainly with a black cloud over his name – to the nearby mining town of Mount Egerton. It proved to be a far cry, if not really a far distance, from Bacchus Marsh.

Back in the day, there were no fly-in-fly-out workers on big salaries standing around in their high-vis vests complaining about the bosses' monstrous salaries and planning their next holiday in Dubai. There were just hundreds of small-scale miners, hoping to strike it big. That meant long, long hours down in pits, digging in the dirt. And when they weren't digging, they were drinking and boasting that they were going to one day be a boss with a monstrous salary. There wasn't much room in their social calendars for matters of the church or what might be described as the leisurely arts of conversation and fine dining.

But Moonlite did find companionship of sorts in Mount Egerton. He managed to track down perhaps the only other two men in the township with any degree of education and interest in matters that did not involve digging and drinking. They were the young bank manager, Ludwig Julius Wilhelm Bruun, and the school teacher, James Simpson. It wasn't quite like Bacchus Marsh soirées, but the three fellows would meet up after work and share some convivial social intercourse. If you know what I mean.

Unfortunately, it didn't last too long. Moonlite and Simpson, the school teacher, soon had a falling out. The causes differ according to who you listen to. The school teacher reckoned that it was due to a loan, but Moonlite reckoned it was because he had called Simpson a coward once when he didn't help protect a woman who was being harassed by a drunken miner. Regardless of the cause of the spat, they were soon not speaking and no longer enjoyed convivial social intercourse with each other.

Understanding their changed relationship is vital to understanding the mystery behind the incident that really started Moonlite's sudden and rapid downward spiral in life: the 1869 robbery of the Mount Egerton Bank – much more famous in its day than the Kelly gang's robberies at Euroa or Jerilderie.

Perhaps, before I tell you about the robbery, I should go into some details about Moonlite's beliefs on social conformity driven by theology and, in particular, the mantle of guilt of the Ten Commandments of the Old Testament. No. Just kidding. Who gives a rat's arse about 19th century theology when we could be talking about a bank robbery? Grand theft auto without the auto! Fasten your seat belt and let's get on with the story.

According to the *Ballarat Star* of Monday 10 May 1869:

DARING BANK ROBBERY AT EGERTON.

On Saturday night, at about ten o'clock, a robbery of a very barefaced character was perpetrated at the Mount Egerton branch of the London Chartered Bank of Australia. A young man, aged about nineteen, named J. W. Bruun, who was in charge of the branch bank there, returned to his office at ten o'clock on Saturday night, after having paid a visit to the township, and was in the act of placing the key in the door, when a man suddenly approached from behind and told him not to kick up a noise, or he would knock him down, at the same time cocking a revolver (supposed to be a Colt's) and placing the muzzle close to the side of the young man's head. The robber then told Bruun to give everything that he had up, and, as he was unarmed and unable to offer resistance in the presence of an armed man, he found himself compelled to comply with the demand.

The masked bandit stole over £2,000 in cash and gold and then led Bruun at gunpoint to the local school house, where he forced him to write a note that read:

> I hereby certify that L. W. Bruun has done everything in his power to withstand this intrusion and the taking away of the money, which was done with firearms.

The robber then signed it: 'Captain Moonlite, Secr.'

So the name and the legend was born. The robber, Captain Moonlite, the professed secretary of some secret society or other, then took a small piece of rope and tied Bruun's wrists together, telling him that he had a mate who would stay outside the school room to watch that Bruun did not escape. But, after the robber had gone, Bruun used a knife hidden in his hat to cut himself free.

He immediately raised the alarm and told the police that he recognised the voice of the robber as that of Scott. He also reported that Scott had once told him that his militia men in New Zealand used to call him Captain Moonlite.

The police brought Scott in for questioning, but he claimed that he had been in a nearby township, seeing a lady whose name he was too much of a gentleman to divulge. He even produced a blurry train ticket to support the story. The police weren't entirely convinced, but they slowly began to notice several things about Bruun's story that seemed just a little bit suspicious to their razor-sharp, highly-trained CSI minds.

For instance, why had young Bruun inexplicably left over £1,000 in the bank, when he should have handed it over to the local police for safekeeping? He also had almost no experience with guns, despite identifying the sound of the gun as that of a Colt. He also claimed that most of the robbery was undertaken in complete darkness, which begs the question, how could the robber see into the safe to make sure that he had removed everything? Also, when the robber took him for a stroll around the township, they encountered two men walking with a lantern. Those men told the police that they had seen Bruun and the other man but did not notice he was masked or holding a gun. Bruun also said that they went past a pub, which he was unable to run into for help because it was closed. Even though it was not. He also said that the robber had him light and hold two separate matches to see by while he wrote the letter that he dictated, and that he held the matches in one hand while writing with the other.

Give that a try some time. It's not quite as hard as trying to get off three rounds in six seconds from the sixth-floor window of the Texas Book Depository in Dallas, but it's almost as difficult.

After freeing himself, Bruun borrowed a horse and rode to the town of Gordon, to the north, to rouse the police there. He accused his friend Scott of being the robber Moonlite, claiming to have recognised him by his voice and his limp, despite having earlier described the robber as 'short of stature and stout, with his face blacked, but whether from colouring or covering over with crape, could not be said.' Scott was neither low nor thickset.

Add to all that the fact that, in Mount Egerton the next morning, the school master James Simpson was running tours of the school room like he was some Foxtel True Crime historian, showing where the robber had tied Bruun up and giving details of the incident that he could not possibly have known – particularly since Bruun was still at Gordon. And the note paper that the 'Moonlite' note had been written on was found to have been torn from a school book that Simpson had taken home on Saturday afternoon.

Further, the police could find no spent matches in the school room, and, on analysing the signature on the note, they found that it bore great similarity to Simpson's handwriting.

Are you seeing anything to raise suspicions? So, on 23 July 1869, Bruun and Simpson were tried at Ballarat by Mr Justice Redmond Barry on the charge of robbing the Mount Egerton Bank. Redmond Barry was the same judge who later sentenced Ned Kelly to death. But this story is not about Ned Kelly, so we are not going to talk about him, right?

Anyway, included among the witnesses for the prosecution was Andrew George Scott, who happily testified against his former friends. Yet both men were ultimately acquitted, on the grounds that there was insufficient evidence against them.

By this time, Scott had already left Mount Egerton in high dudgeon because of accusations of being a bank robber. Strangely enough, he seemed to have had extra money in his pockets to splash about.

My own theory is that Simpson and Bruun planned and conducted the robbery, but Moonlite guessed where they had hidden the money and gold and took it for himself.

If Moonlite taught me anything, it was to take advantage of opportunities that were there for the taking.

- - -

The tropical splendour of Fiji

After leaving Melbourne, Moonlite used the sudden funds in his pockets to journey to Fiji aboard the vessel *Pilot*. He carried with him a letter of introduction from a friend in Bacchus Marsh, commending him as a solid chap and a good chum and so on. Such letters were pretty important if you didn't have your own website to show who you were.

On the voyage, Moonlite met the owner of the ship, Allan Hughan, and they became good chums too. Upon reaching Fiji, Hughan introduced Moonlite to a business friend, Francis Holworthy. The men hit it off and decided to establish a cotton plantation together in nearby New Caledonia.

Moonlite clearly fell in love with the tropical splendour of Fiji and the freedom he found there, because he purchased the small island of Vomo off the north-east coast. Well, when I say purchased – he started the transaction, and provided a promissory note for £260, but never actually paid for it. The dream of that island stayed with him, though. It seemed to be the place he escaped to in his head when the slings and arrows of outrageous fortune assaulted him. It was the place that he promised us we would all escape to, to live the lives we deserved to live.

Anyway, Moonlite used the funds that Holworthy provided him with to purchase cotton seed and equipment and sailed off to Sydney – via New Caledonia, where he ran up some unpaid bills for accommodation and drinks. He arrived in New South Wales with another letter of introduction, this one from Holworthy to one Alfred Hilder, stating that he was a solid chap and good chum and sound business partner, etc.

So, in Sydney he's drinking and partying like some rugby league dickhead, splashing cash around freely. He had also gone to the Sydney Mint to sell 120 ounces of gold, remarkably similar in size to the gold that went missing from Mount Egerton. He received about £550 for the gold and then deposited another £200 into the bank, which he used to draw cheques upon. Lots of cheques! Then lots more cheques! All the while, letters were coming from Holworthy and Hughan, asking why they had not heard from him. His relationship with the married Hughan was perhaps 'fleshed out' a little in a note that the elder man sent him from Fiji, reading in part:

> My little heart's treasure, my joyous innocent darling, I would rather see you than anyone on earth

Late in 1870, Moonlite's bank account was declared empty, and he promptly left Sydney and went up to Maitland, near Newcastle, to buy supplies with cheques that bounced like rubber balls going down concrete steps. Then he returned to Sydney and bought a small yacht aptly called the *Why Not,* as his last chance to escape the debtors and flee back to Fiji, or wherever he planned to escape to. He paid for the yacht with another cheque. This one was made out for £130, which was so large and bounced so high that even the police saw it.

Imagine the scene: there was Moonlite, scuttling through the early morning streets of Sydney, with bills unpaid even at the boarding house where he'd been staying, ready to cast off and head out of the harbour into the open sea, tacking his way against the winds of pursuing debts.

In one telling of the story, he has a young woman on his arm. In another, he is quite alone. Either way, he had barely sailed outside the harbour heads when a police launch came up behind him to intercept the yacht. They boarded and arrested Moonlite for his many bad debts. Of course, he protested his innocence, looking towards the wide horizon out there before him. He declared that there was a scoundrel in the city, a German Count Geldern, passing off bad cheques in his name, and if they let him go, the *Current Affairs* reporters would surely track down the actual rogue and prove his innocence.

But they weren't having any of it. They dragged him back to shore and put him before a court, which sentenced him to 18 months in Maitland Gaol. According to the *Town and Country Journal* of 1879:

> And here we hear of his first crime, for soon after his arrival he was sentenced on 20th and 21st December, 1870, at Darlinghurst sittings, to 18 months' imprisonment in Maitland Gaol for uttering a cheque... The first false step was made, and the downward career had begun.

He only served 15 months, though, after a clever or crazy scheme to show he was insane – or just his inevitable character – saw him lodged in the Sydney Asylum for a while before being transferred to the Parramatta Gaol. Released in early 1872, he was actually collecting his possessions from the prison authorities when the long arm of the law reached out and grabbed him yet again, charging him with robbing the Mount Egerton Bank. His old chums, Bruun and Simpson, had not been idle while he was up in Sin-City, and were busy collecting evidence and spite and vengeance to pass on to the police to show that Scott was the real robber. Bruun became particularly obsessed with tracking down the good Captain, my Captain. He hired a private investigator, again aptly named, George Sly. And we all know, there have always been a lot of sly private investigators in Sydney, right.

Sly was a very competent investigator, in fact, and soon discovered Moonlite's trail – tracking him down to Sydney and finding him in Parramatta Gaol. He helped the Victorian police build up quite a case against Scott, who was rearrested and extradited to Victoria to face a reopening of the Mount Egerton Bank Robbery trial.

My belief is that Bruun and Simpson had tracked him down to get the stolen money back. When they found it all spent on wine, women and song (well, the song is uncertain, and the women speculation, but certainly a lot was spent on wine and other alcohol), they turned nasty.

So he was sent down to Ballarat Gaol – but he escaped. This is starting to sound like a Sunday afternoon movie, I know. But it's true. He dug a tunnel out of his cell, got into another cell and, from there, broke out into the corridor. Then he grabbed the warder and put him in a cell and took his keys and let dozens of prisoners free. It's a good ploy, and worth making a note of – if you want to escape, you need to take lots of people with you – so the police are busy chasing the dumber ones, while you get away.

And that's exactly what he did. It was just like the Great Escape. They dug a tunnel under the outer wall, from one of the Stalag Huts, or they hid the digging teams under a wooden horse they'd built for exercising in the yard, or they all dressed up as cleaning women and snuck out past the German guards, all looking like Richard Attenborough or Steve McQueen in turns. Most of the other prisoners were captured and taken to a field and shot with machine guns hidden in the back of a truck, though. Or not.

The Ballarat Gaol escape made newspaper headlines as far away as Queensland, with the *Brisbane Courier* saying:

> It is conjectured by the officers of the gaol that the six planned the escape under the tutelage of Moonlite, and that they are probably bent on bushranging, with Moonlite as their 'Brother Devil.'

The reporter castigated the quality of building materials used in the gaol. Stating that while the popular idea was that gaol cells were impregnable, he said the prison had either been constructed 'in the days when bricks and mortar were either not very good, or architects were unskilful, or contractors were scamps'.

The report stated:

> Instead of the cell doors being made of good thick iron, they are made of soft wood, covered over on the inside with the thinnest sheet iron we have ever seen. It is about as thick as brown paper, and once punctured, can be torn off as easily as one may tear a sheet of zinc.

He also criticised the prison guard, Mr Irwin, who was assaulted by the escaping prisoners, because his statement differed significantly from other accounts:

> Irwin complains of hurts in the mouth, and his description of the struggle with Scott and Plunkett indicates a terrific combat of wrestling forces, but he has happily come out of the fray without much to show for his part in the business.

Anyway, Moonlite was eventually recaptured and returned to prison. He appeared in front of Redmond Barry, and we won't mention the Ned bloody Kelly connection this time, but his court case was memorable for the way he defended himself and tied the prosecutor in circles. I think that he might have gotten off on another day, or if he'd had a QC defending him, or had been a member of the Melbourne Club, or had been a company executive or politician or so on. Redmond Barry, however, clearly knew the difference between white-collar and clergy-collar crime.

He was an interesting character himself, quite a root rat in his youth – and both an arch conservative and generous to the poor and needy. But he could be harsh to those he thought represented a menace to the pillars of society or who threatened to show him up in court with more eloquent speech and rhetoric.

He found Moonlite repeatedly guilty of upstaging him and sentenced him to ten years' hard labour in Pentridge. Moonlite continued to protest his innocence. Even in his death cell, years later, when he was finally making a clean breast of things, he maintained his innocence of the Mount Egerton Bank robbery – so you have to presume there was truth in that. Maybe.

- - -

Life in Pentridge

Despite what Moonlite told us about his time in Pentridge – that life was harsh, and he had spent time in solitary for bad behaviour after falling in with a very rough crowd that he learned to protect himself from by using his wits, and that he slowly won the respect of both prisoners and gaolers – there is another story out there in what they call the public domain. You could find it, if you knew where to look, but don't presume that it can be found easily. And of course it's on the web – which is just as big a cop out as saying something is in the public domain. (Excuse me, I'm looking for information on how to fill out this bloody government form because it doesn't make any sense to me. Oh, it's all on the web. Or, could you send me some information on assistance for my kids whose dad left us and we don't know what we should do. Don't worry, it's all on the web. Yeah, and the lucky four-leaf clover is in the field of clovers, and the needle is in the haystack, and gold is at the end of the rainbow, and the plans for building an intergalactic bypass through Earth are on display in the planning office on Alpha Centauri).

But if you know how to look up old newspapers online in archives, you might have a chance of finding this story. While Moonlite was in Pentridge prison, a scurrilous tabloid journalist, who went by the pen name of the Vagabond, decided to sneak into the prison and write a series of exposés. If he'd had a video camera, he would have sold the footage to *A Current Affair* or some other trashy TV show, but all he had was a pen and paper and his eyes. And, of course, his imagination.

The man's real name was John Stanley Thomas, although he also went by the name of Julian Thomas, and he wrote for a dozen different papers. His thang was to don a disguise and get access to lunatic asylums, hospitals or churches, and then write up his experience as a great exposé. He spent one month in Pentridge,

Pentridge Gaol (SLV)

working as a dispenser of medicines in the prison hospital. And no, he had no qualifications as such, and who knows what medicines he dispensed to the poor prisoners who fronted up.

Well, he determined that the two prisoners most in need of his journalistic services, dispensing a dose of hypocrisy and half-truths, were Moonlite and Harry Power. Power, to save you Googling him, was the man who had taken a very young Ned Kelly under his wing and apprenticed him in the fine arts of bushranging. Think of him as a very cranky and surly Donald Trump. He had taken a young Ned up into the mountains and showed him his hideouts and taught him the rudiments of bushranging.

There are some who said that Ned dobbed him in to the police after Power tried to make him his best boy. Anyway, I digress. The Vagabond described Moonlite as 'one of the celebrities of Pentridge' and wrote:

> He is a dashing, smart, rather cunning-looking young man, of about 30 years of age. His education gives him a superiority over the other prisoners, who also respect him for his crimes, and he has become a sort of leader among them. He is a regular 'prison lawyer', and is full of quibbles and quirks, and has proved himself, I believe, quite a terror and nuisance to Mr. Gardiner, the superintendent. I don't think that Scott was quite judiciously treated at first. Petty punishments and annoyances appear to have been freely dealt out to him as to others. He has chafed against these, and has lately broken out into more dangerous breaches of discipline.

The Vagabond was further creating the myth of Moonlite and wrote of him as a bit delusional, as saying that he had friends in high places who could have any of the authorities sacked from their positions. Thomas was a fine one to talk, though, for his own delusions were evident throughout his writing. He perpetually peppered his stories with fictitious imaginings about himself, implying that he had fought in the American Civil War, that he had been an officer leading large numbers of men, that he had once had a fling with Kylie Minogue – you know the type.

Anyway, his deep psychological insight, based largely on one conversation, diagnosed Moonlite:

> I don't know that Captain Moonlite is exactly a man of criminal instincts. He must, however, have had tendencies that way, for with

his education and early training should certainly not have gone wrong. His, however seems one of these natures fond of adventure and of wild life which revolt at the restraints of civilization. He might have made a good sailor, and would have been a good comrade in a filibustering expedition. With judicious treatment I think he might have been re-claimed. But at present there is no doubt that he is a very dangerous man. He is essentially vain, and is fond of the admiration of the 'lifers' and other hardened ruffians. I do not think Captain Moonlite's personality so dangerous as in the example set to and influence he exerts over others.

Another Pentridge story is that Moonlite may well have met Ned Kelly there. You only need to look at their dates of their imprisonment and note that Kelly would have been a brash 18-year-old, serving time for receiving a stolen horse while Moonlite was there. If they did meet, Moonlite would never admit to it. Perhaps, one theory goes, he tried to befriend the young hothead, who rejected him, starting Moonlite's feud with the Kellys. We'll never know. When asked about who he met in Pentridge, he would only say that the person of most consequence was fellow prisoner James Nesbitt.

- - -

Released from prison

Moonlite was eventually released from prison in 1879, having served seven years of his ten year sentence. He returned to society with James Nesbitt in tow and a scheme to earn a crust as a public speaker. With the help of a journalist and theatrical agent, Richard Thatcher, he advertised a series of lectures on law reform and on the evils of the prison system. His stories would probably have made good fodder for an episode of *Underbelly*, but the police kept closing down his lectures. The one good thing that came from them was that, in recruiting assistants to help him, he met most of us boys.

You should have seen him in those days. He had this booming great confidence that spread out from him like a bright light and encompassed you. When he sat down beside you, and maybe put an arm on your arm, and told you how he was going to change society and how we'd be a part of it – why, we would have lain down to stop traffic on the Bolte Bridge for him.

As the esteemed writer from the *Town and Country Journal* put it:

> Scott is a man of commanding presence, is highly educated, and his manners are gentlemanly and winning. Brave to the verge of recklessness, cool, clear headed, and sagacious, and with a certain air of chivalrous dash, he is the *beau ideal* of a brigand chief. He is a man who would exercise sovereign power over untrained and uneducated, and especially youthful minds, while the fascination of his manner would secure him adherents and friends anywhere. The man's indomitable will, splendid intellect and fascinating manner, render him more dangerous to the community than a dozen ordinary bushrangers.

You can see why we loved him so much, can't you.

He was often writing up the notes for his lectures, always refining them and pacing around practising them. He had this thing about getting the words just right in a way that could sort of weave a spell over the audience. It's hard to explain now, but he had a way of telling a story that really sucked you in. It was all about getting the rhythm and cadences and words to resonate with a person's inner conscience, he said. I don't know about that, but the way he talked was pretty powerful. You just wanted to keep him talking, to hear more and more of it.

If he'd been able to give his lectures, I'm sure they'd be box set Xmas specials at Kmart that wouldn't be discounted in January. They'd be something everyone wanted to listen to and replay and listen to again. But he never got to give them, did he. The police kept finding ways to have his lectures cancelled. They'd tell the venue that they feared a disturbance and violence. They'd tell the hall owners that a bomb threat had been called in, and they had to evacuate everyone. Or they'd just tell them that Moonlite was actually a lewd burlesque performer whose lectures involved unspeakable acts with animals and small children.

Bastards!

- - -

Introducing the gang

So we're nearly done with the back story now, and close to being able to say again, so here we were, sneaking out of Melbourne. But, first, let me finally get around to introducing you to the gang. We, those 'untrained, uneducated and youthful minds'.

The number one boy, who Moonlite called Number One at Wantabadgery Station when he was trying to protect our identities from those we held at gunpoint, was of course James Nesbitt. He had met Moonlite in Pentridge, where he was serving four years under the name of James Lyon, for robbery with violence. His prison photos show a gentle-faced lad with a large round chin and a bit of a stunned look on his face – as if he couldn't really understand how he got there. And, in another world, he wouldn't have. He was basically an innocent soul who always thought the best of others – regardless. Some might think him a bit naïve, or a bit of a dill, but he honestly did not expect to be caught and convicted, because he was stealing to support his mother and sister. In so many ways, he was the balance to Moonlite's erratic and violent temperament. When you saw them together, you could understand the attraction. He claimed to be 19 years old, though we never knew if he was maybe adding a few years or subtracting them.. Based on his photo, you'd have to cast Mark Wahlberg to play him in the movie.

According to the *Argus* newspaper:

> Nesbitt's career in crime up to the present has been somewhat slight in comparison to that of other desperadoes who have taken to the 'pistol and pad'. He is known to the police as James Lyons, alias Nesbitt, and he was born in Buninyong in 1857. He professes to be a Roman Catholic. His height is 5ft. 9½in., his build being of a medium

Moonlite and his gang

Clockwise from top: Moonlite (SLV), James Nesbitt (SLV), Thomas Rogan (NSW SA&R), Thomas Williams (NSW SA&R), Gus Wernicke (Australasian Sketcher), Graham Bennett (NSW SA&R)

order, his complexion fresh, and his hair dark brown. In July, 1873, he received a sentence of one month's imprisonment, with hard labour, for larceny. In September of the same year he was sentenced to three months' imprisonment for a similar offence, and in July, 1875, he was sentenced to four years' imprisonment for assault and robbery.

Number Two was Thomas Rogan, who sometimes went by the name of Thomas Baker. The best way to describe him was as an angry young man. He was swarthy, with a thickset brow and the type of features that might have been considered possibly Aboriginal enough to prompt police to pull him over and check the car's rego papers just because. Like Nesbitt, he had been previously convicted of larceny and horse stealing (Grand Theft Auto of the day). He had been brutalised by his time in prison and never much wanted to talk about it. He was big on tough talk though, until things got a bit rough, when the bullets started flying, he began crying like a girl and hid. He was 21 and could probably be played by Jason Momoa, not because he physically looked anything like him, but because he could do the frown right and he'd guarantee a good audience, right?

Number Three was Thomas Williams, who also went by the names Frank Johns or Charlie Davidson. He joined Moonlite after applying for the position of secretary to assist him with his lecture tours at Ballarat. He had a bit of education and also had hopes for a future far outside Ballarat. The job was a ticket out of the town for him, as well as out of the reach of a domineering father and mother who wanted him to become an accountant or an actuary or a clerk or something safe and boring.

Despite not receiving any salary because the lectures were a failure, he followed Moonlite back to Melbourne and moved into the boarding house in Atherton Street, Fitzroy, where Moonlite and Nesbitt lived. Atherton Street later became a bit of a slum, inhabited by migrants, the marginalised and long-term unemployed, until the houses were bulldozed in the 1960s and replaced by high-rise housing commission flats – which, dare I say it, have become inhabited largely these days by migrants, the marginalised and the long-term unemployed. Williams was 19 years old and had a long, thin face and well-kept hair. he could be played by one Mark Wahlberg's lesser-known brothers.

Number Four was Gus Wernicke – also known as Warnecky, Wrenkie, Wernicke, Warneckie and every other variation that journalists settled on while only bothering half-arsedly to spell his name right. He was only 15 years old, although he told people that he was 19. His father was a publican who owned two hotels in

Melbourne, both running brothels out of them. Wernicke was found by Moonlite living in one of the brothels, in a poor state. The lad told him that he had not eaten anything that day, so Moonlite took him for coffee and buns. Wernicke told him that he had been employed in a plumber's shop in Little Bourke Street, where he got five shillings a week, but he was flogged after losing half a sovereign and had run away. Moonlite immediately told him that he could find lodgings with him and his boys.

Wernicke was angry that his father neglected him, angry that he had left him to live the life that he did, and was even angry at Moonlite at times – threatening to leave him. But we all knew he never would. There is one surviving sketch of him, standing by a chair. His head looks a little too big for his body, and you'd wonder whether Mark Wahlberg has any kids old enough to play him.

Finally, Number Five was me – Graham Bennett, with no other aliases other than Number Five. I was 18 years old, a Sagittarian who attended The Derek Zoolander School for Kids Who Can't Read Good and Want to Do Other Stuff Good Too. My favourite bands are the Living End and Leonard Cohen, and my favourite shows are *Breaking Bad, Sons of Anarchy* and *True Lies*. My Facebook profile picture doesn't show my handsome, clean-shaven face with dark hair combed neatly across my forehead, rather, it shows the skull of a horse on a fence post.

Keep 'em guessing, right?

- - -

We'll be keeping an eye on you lad!

When Moonlite left prison, the police promised him: 'We'll be keeping an eye on you lad!' And they certainly did. It reached the point where Moonlite and Nesbitt were being accused of every minor or major crime committed around Melbourne, the same way that the Kelly gang were being accused of every crime being committed in the north of the colony. You know the song, 'Someone stole old Banyon's pig. Blame it on the Kellys!' Some of these were clearly attempts at harassment by the police, some were stories started by the press, and some were just crazy ideas put forward by hysterical members of the public caught up in the tabloid excitement of it all. The pair had barely left Pentridge when the harassment started.

At first, the accusations were harmless enough, being easily disproved. Moonlite had robbed a post office somewhere miles from Melbourne, or had stolen a baby from its pram outside the shops, or had rolled a wino in some back alley, or created that email scam about making a fortune from unclaimed millions in Nigeria that just needed to be parked in your bank account for a short period.

Then they started getting silly. Moonlite had killed a Chinaman at Merri Creek and robbed his market garden. Moonlite was shoplifting DVDs and selling them on street corners. Eventually, they became more serious – such as, they had murdered an actor named Mr Bates. That was clever thinking by the police, because actors are always considered more important celebrities than politicians or other public figures. Moonlite was put into a line up over that one, along with a motley crew of drunken slobs. Moonlite, the only well-dressed one among them, stood out like a cock on a hen, of course. But he got off by undermining the credibility of the lone police witness they'd dragged out of the drunk tank for the identification. I'll give him that, he was very sharp and eloquent when focused. But I guess the coppers were trying to rattle his focus.

And the harassment continued. He was accused of attempting to attack the Williamstown battery and free some convicts there. The newspapers were full of it, giving great details of the plans and inventing imaginary plots about how he wanted to form a gang and join up with the Kellys in the north. Police Superintendent Sadleir claimed: 'Scott sent word to Ned Kelly that he wished to join forces with him.'

That really rattled people. It notched up the hysteria to another level – though anyone who knew what he thought of the Kellys knew how ludicrous that was.

Then he and Nesbitt were hauled in again and charged with robbing a bank in Lancefield, over 100 miles north of Melbourne. Their pictures were even dispatched to the site for verification, but the bank workers admitted that they did not look like the robbers – who were, anyway, soon discovered with the stolen money.

The papers lapped up every new and more ridiculous story. His activities were selling like a royal family sex scandal. Each new accusation was printed in larger bold headlines, but the eventual retractions were hidden up the back, beyond the shipping news, near the old junk for sale and public notices where only the lonely hearts searchers would stumble upon it. Yet, each time the media coverage reached new levels of hysteria, Moonlite and Nesbitt were asked to leave their accommodation as undesirable clients.

The only recourse for Moonlite and Nesbitt was to leave the colony. But, if they attempted to do that, they would be in breach of their early release conditions and they would be reimprisoned. And you can't tell me the police didn't know that. They were determined to put him back behind bars, one way or the other.

Bastards! (Did I mention that already?)

- - -

What pissed him off even more

The police harassment was bad, but do you know what pissed him off even more? The talk of the Kelly gang! They were still getting good coverage – Ned Kelly this and Ned Kelly that – even though the gang hadn't been seen in ages. It was like they had a booking agent who was advising them not to overexpose their image. And that's where Moonlite saw his chance, I think. He figured he could ride through the gap they'd left, become the number one bad-ass bushranger in the land and be the conversation topic in all the drawing rooms and all the clubs and pubs everywhere.

Which just goes to show one of the contradictions in his character. He'd rant whenever the papers wrote about him, and he'd rant whenever they wrote about the Kellys instead of him. Were the Kelly gang hiding out in the mountains? Had they crossed over into New South Wales? Had they snuck away to New Zealand? If four unknown men on horseback were sighted anywhere, there was an immediate suspicion that they were the Kellys. In March of 1879, the newspapers reported that a gang of fellows 'very much resembling the Kelly gang' had been seen encamped on Pentil Island, on the Murray River.

Then, in June, the *Wagga Wagga Advertiser* claimed to have information from private sources that the Kelly gang were expected in the Bourke district *en route* to the Queensland border. A posse of police, with Indigenous trackers, were dispatched to intercept them. At the same time, the ship *Alexandra*, departing from Victoria for Newcastle, was found to have four extra men on board. Telegrams went to Newcastle, seeking to have the vessel boarded to make sure that they were not the Kellys.

Perhaps it was just his celebrity ranking. For example, when two men robbed the Lancefield bank, north of Melbourne, in August, newspapers reported that they were 'supposed to be the Kellys'. That didn't prove to be the case, so the press and police dropped to their B list, stating: 'an impression now prevails that the robbers were Scott, alias Captain Moonlite, and Nesbitt, and not the Kellys'.

You should have seen him storming back from the newsagency with a paper under his arm, waiting for an audience, so he could point at the offending article and rant about the injustice of it – waving the paper in the air about his head like he was up on a podium urging parliament to grant marriage to gays or to ban poker machines. He'd read it out word for word and scoff at the ignorance of the press and the gullibility of reporters in general. All the while, he'd ask rhetorical questions that we were never sure whether we were meant to answer.

'Do they think we are capable of being in two places at once?' he'd demand. And Rogan would look across at Nesbitt for any indication of whether he was meant to answer the question, since Scott might be staring at him fixedly. And Nesbitt might shrug, as if he didn't quite know either, and before either of them could figure it out, he'd be firing another question at them: 'Can you tell me how a man is meant to maintain his state of mind with such scurrilous reports being printed about him repeatedly?'

If he'd pause, as if he really was expecting an answer, the boys would lick their lips, like they were getting ready to say something, but were really just waiting for one of the others to say it first, all hoping that Moonlite would relaunch into his rant before demanding an answer from any one of them. It was worse than being in school, in some ways.

But he'd calm down eventually, or Nesbitt would get up and make a cup of tea and bring it to him, and Moonlite would be struck by the kindness of the gesture and would put his arm around Nesbitt and declare that he was in the company of true friends, and that would carry a man through all adversities. And then he'd fling the newspaper into the fire and sit down with his cup of tea. But you could bet he hadn't cast the annoyance aside. His eyes would be like blue ice, glaring into the depths of his tea cup, so you'd think it might turn the boiled water chill again.

- - -

The Fiji story

A story started circulating around then, suggesting that Moonlite was planning to steal a steamer and take it to Fiji. It was a pretty plausible story, actually, if you put all the other robberies and fancies together. The money from the robbery at Lancefield would bankroll them, and the extra men they freed from the Williamstown battery would be needed for the theft – and they could even use the vegetables from the Chinaman's market garden they robbed to maintain levels of roughage to keep them regular. With six men, they would take passage on a mail steamer. Three armed men would hold the native crew at gunpoint, one more would keep the deck crew captive, and Moonlite and one other would take over the bridge. Only one officer would be kept to navigate the boat. All the others, along with the passengers, would be put into open boats and sent on their way.

There would be plenty of gold boxes on the ship, going from the diggings to a bank somewhere or other. With that gold in hand, they would sail to Fiji, or South America, or some remote place where they could live the life of celebrity bandits in exile, like Ronald Biggs, engaged in whatever 'heinous' practices the courts and newspapers of the time only hinted at.

It is hard to say whether it was Moonlite's own idea to leave the colony, or whether police accusations led to it. Anyway, around 1879, he determined that he would have no peace until he left Melbourne. He began telling us what a different life could be like. Sitting in cold boarding house rooms, knowing we had as little chance of paying our rent as to affording a good meal, how could we not follow his dreams too?

- - -

Andrew Scott, Moonlite, wood carving by Alfred May and Alfred Martin Ebsworth (SLV)

The gorilla in the room, not the elephant

Okay, it's time to talk about the gorilla in the room. And let's get one thing clear – a gorilla is not an elephant! The elephant in the room is the analogy of different people going into a darkened room and each touching a different part of the elephant and concluding that it was a different animal. The one who touched the tail called it a donkey, the one who touched the trunk thought it was a snake, and the one who touched the foot believed that it was a hippopotamus. And so on. The gorilla in the room is the thing that nobody wants to talk about.

And the gorilla in this room is the allegations of Moonlite's homosexuality.

You think it might have been easier being gay in the good old days? I mean, it wasn't something you could see as easily in how people dressed, and you certainly didn't see any blokes swanning about in the parklands or walking along St Kilda Road in high heels and makeup being shouted at by bogans in passing cars. You couldn't tell from looking at anyone whether they might be gay or not, and it wasn't until they got behind closed doors that they might exhibit what they felt in their heart. But that wasn't easier at all. It was much harder. It was considered a sin that was carried deep within. It was the love that dared not speak its name, to quote Oscar Wilde's lover, Bosie.

In April 1872, for instance, Moonlite was 30 years old and had just been arrested in Sydney for the Mount Egerton Bank Robbery. While he was planning his breakout from the Ballarat Gaol, a young man named Edward Feeney was sentenced to death in Melbourne for the murder of another young man, his close friend Charles Marks. Feeney was arrested in the Treasury Gardens, smoking a cigar and sitting morosely next to the body of Marks, who had been shot in the chest.

Evidence at his trial suggested that it wasn't just your average, garden variety murder. Feeney and Marks had attempted a double suicide, each holding the muzzle of a pistol to the chest of the other man. Feeney successfully shot his friend Marks, but Marks did not shoot him – possibly because of a fault with the gun, but possibly also because he lost his resolve.

It didn't take long for the press to intimate that they were lovers. Indeed, the *Argus* referred to a witness who had known the two men:

> and he observed also that there was an unusual fondness on the part of Marks towards Feeney, more like that of a man for a woman or a woman for a man, than that which usually subsists between even intimate friends of the same sex.

Feeney was found guilty of murder and executed. His post-mortem was witnessed by the governor of the Melbourne Gaol, J. B. Castieau, who wrote in his diary:

> There was a Post-Mortem held after the usual Inquest and the Medical Students under the direction of Dr Barker revelled in the luxury of a fresh and healthy corpse. 'Oh poor humanity' how small you look on the dissecting table. There had been some strange stories told of the connection that existed between Feeney and the murdered man. Barker exposed Feeney's rectum and both he and Dr Youl said it told of a vicious indulgence. I was asked my opinion…to coincide with theirs but I declined as I had no experience of what a healthy rectum would represent.

The story is sad enough, of course, but there's a bloody Ned Kelly link to it. Why is there always a bloody Ned Kelly link to things? Castieau was still governor at the gaol when Ned Kelly was hanged there in 1880. More than that, his young son Godfrey was taken to see Ned in his death cell. Ned made such an impression on the young lad that, when he went on to become an actor, using the stage name Godfrey Cass, he actually played Ned Kelly in 1920 and 1923 in two of the earliest films about him.

But there was an early film made about Moonlite too, do you know? It was made in 1910 – but, like the truth about Moonlite, it is largely lost to us. Only a few minutes of footage remain, showing two appallingly dressed white guys, trying to pass themselves off as Chinese, while a bushranger robs them. Another scene is more memorable for having the full shadow of the camera operator across it. The film's director, John Gavin, played the main role. His wife Agnes, with her face blackened, played an Aboriginal woman. Very classy stuff.

Gavin actually released two bushranger films in 1910, cashing in on a mini boom in bushranger films such as *Captain Midnight* and *Captain Starlight* that were touring the country. Gavin's other film was *Thunderbolt*. He portrayed bushrangers as violent and fierce, and he also treated the police force with contempt. His Moonlite film, though, was as much based on Rolf Boldrewood's *Robbery Under Arms* as it was on Moonlite's life – but with the addition of a love plot and a gold escort robbery, and with Moonlite giving some of the money to the poor. It was considered quite a box office hit at the time. The producer even boasted of it as: 'A bushranging saga in the grand manner, with enough dead troopers to warrant a severe censorship.' He was right in that, as bushranging films were banned in New South Wales and Victoria in 1912 for some years, because of the negative portrayal of police and the focus on criminal activities.

But is the Moonlite film on the list of UNESCO World Heritage items like the first Kelly film? I hardly need to ask, do I. Of course not. Has it been remade, starring anyone from the Hollywood A list, and made a gazillion dollars? Of course not, again. But Moonlite fandom has led to a couple of Indy productions (which is short form for rather artsy, yet you won't have much chance of finding them, even on Pirate Bay).

I found them, though, and I thought they weren't too bad, but what would I know, right?

- - -

Finally sneaking out of Melbourne

So here we were, finally sneaking out of Melbourne, led on by Moonlite's stories, his words the pavers of a yellow-brick road before us. We were now members of a gang of notorious bushrangers – even though none of us except Moonlite knew how to either ride a horse or fire a gun. But never let the facts ruin a good story, right? You listening, *Town and Country Journal?*

We can skip the journey north across the colony of Victoria, except to say that it was a painfully slow trek. We ended up selling some of our clothing for food when we couldn't get work anywhere. We shot a few native bears – which is what we called koalas then – and some sheep at times too. The sheep were better eating.

I think the journey weighed heavily on Moonlite. He was risking re-imprisonment by attempting to leave the colony, and he had to carry all our fears and anxieties deep in his bags, with the manuscripts of his lecture tours. I used to wonder about all those lecture tour notes. What demons was he exorcising in them? What drove him to write? What was the dark inner ink from which he gathered his words? Or perhaps he just carried them from fear that discovering that if he didn't have them – if they were lost – it wouldn't actually make any discernible difference?

The further we travelled, the better and better became the stories he told to us. He told us how easy life in Fiji was going to be. How we'd be a big family with our own servants, living in a large wooden house overlooking the ocean and how we'd feed on fish and exotic fruits while we watched our crops and wealth grow there around us. And the scent of the islands would be warm and damp, with a taste to it, like vegetables being cooked in a pot wrapped in a cloth.

And when you approach the land from the sea, late in the evening, the sun strikes the water in such a way that it shimmers and dances like silver. Then, when you walk through arrivals and customs, a group of men greet you singing Fijian songs on their guitars – that half sad, half joyful island wail, calling you back to a place you will one day call home.

The more he talked about it, the more real it became to us. And with that came an increasing need to prevent anybody from ever taking the dream away from us.

- - -

Did I mention the Kellys?

Then there were also the Kellys, following us the whole length of our journey – or, at least, following Moonlite. I knew it the day we passed a travelling merchant who stopped his dray as we approached him and asked nervously: 'Who are you? You're not the Kellys are you?'

I saw the look on Moonlite's face. He might have shot him on the spot for that, except that Nesbitt put his hand on his arm and led him on. That's when he decided that, if we were going to be labelled as bushrangers, we might as well act like them. He started drilling us in the use of firearms, using the few old guns he carried. He was a crack shot, though. He would line up stones or chunks of wood on a log and, making it look so easy, shooting each one off in turn.

'It's a far different thing to point a gun at a man and fire, though,' he'd say, telling us how he'd shot down ferocious Māori, Italians and Confederate troops. 'A man looks you in the eye,' he'd say. 'And that's a much harder thing to face than even the fact that he's pointing his own gun back at you.'

We blazed away at the rocks and stones, not paying his words the heed we should have. But young men are always slow to learn except through their errors, right?

As we got near Mansfield, near where the Kelly gang had killed three policemen at Stringybark Creek the year before, we decided to become the Kellys. So we demanded food and guns and ammunition from homesteads we passed.

It got so silly that the Inspecting Superintendent of Police, John Sadlier – who was later to make a complete ass of himself at Kelly's last shoot-out at Glenrowan, turning and running with a minor wound as the first shots were fired – claimed that Moonlite and his gang had sent word to the Kelly gang, asking them to join forces. However, when Ned heard this, the story goes that he sent a message back saying that if Scott or his band approached him, he would shoot them down. It seems that the admiration between the men was fairly mutual.

But we're not going to talk about the Kellys, right?

- - -

Reaching the Murray River

We reached the Murray River in late Spring, and it was this wide, sluggish, muddy thing that looked like anything except a river. Moonlite said that we shouldn't go near the town of Albury, where we'd be sure to be caught. We'd need to cross somewhere up or down river of the town. They'd built the first bridge over the river at Albury about 20 years previously, and the trains ran nearly all the way to the river on the Victorian side, even though there was no train yet on the New South Wales side. And when it did arrive, a few years later, it was a different gauge rail, so people still had to get out and cross over on foot. And prior to all that, you either had to rely on ferrymen with punts or be prepared to get your boots wet.

Now I'd like to tell you that we encountered a strange ferryman with a long white beard and robes like Gandalf, who rowed us across in this old punt, one at a time, and told us each a special message about our future. Or dropped these wonderful and poignant metaphors about moving from one colony to the next being like crossing into a different reality in some way. And you can believe that if you want to. Or you can believe that we nearly drowned and were only saved by Moonlite. I mean, these types of metaphorical crossings need to be tough, right?

But we just waded across the muddy river, holding onto logs to support ourselves, and emerged like wet mangy dogs needing to shake ourselves dry, with Victoria there behind us as our ill past, and New South Wales there ahead of us as our better future.

What were we thinking?

There is another story that you might find reference to if you go searching, one that goes something like this: we continued in the direction of Wagga Wagga but were forced to keep travelling, because jobs were very scarce. During this time, another man joined the group. His name was Graham Bennett. He had been born in England in 1859, took up sailing as a career and eventually arrived in Australia in 1877. It is believed that he came to try his luck on the goldfields but, having failed, sought work firstly in north-east Victoria and then in New South Wales.

But believe of me what you want, 'cause I'm not telling.

- - -

New South Wales, where everything went to shit

So we had crossed into the Colony of New South Wales, which looked nothing like any part of Wales. It looked remarkably similar to the colony of Victoria, in fact, which just goes to show my ignorance in not seeing how clearly different the two colonies actually were! We kept asking Moonlite, like bored and petulant children on a car trip, 'Are we there yet? Are we there yet?' And he only responded by saying we had a little way to go still, but not too far, telling us that he had a property a little way ahead where we could call in for supplies and a rest.

But, of course, we then reached Wantabadgery, and everything went to shit.

The station there had a reputation as a place where men in need could get some assistance. Until recently, a generous Mr Windeyer had owned it. Remember that surname – we'll hear it again in the courts in Sydney. But that hospitality changed when the station changed hands. A Mr McDonald now owned it, but a stingy, flint-hearted overseer named William Baynes effectively ran it.

Anyway – we were heading east towards the station when we stopped at the home of the nearby McGlede family to ask for work. Although there was nothing there for us, they kindly gave us bread and milk. We would repay them with very bitter currency later, it turned out. We next stopped at a store owned by a Mr Weir. Once again, we asked for work or food, but all he could give us was eight pounds of flour – which is only 3.5 kilograms if you don't talk pounds. Feeling tired, hungry and dejected, we headed on to Wantabadgery station.

In describing the land thereabouts, the *Argus* newspaper reporter, who clearly longed to be a home renovation writer, had said:

> This station is 15 miles in length by eight in breadth. The house is situated on the north bank of the Murrumbidgee, and on an extensive

flat studded with trees like an English park. The country around is hilly, and there is plenty of timber about, but compared with the Kelly district [yeah, I know, I know] in Victoria it is open, and can he traversed easily in any direction on horseback. The house is one story, a new building, of brick and slate, with gardens in front and on the west side. The kitchen and storerooms and a fence form a quadrangular backyard. There is another yard on the east side, in which there are a bathroom, a laundry, and groom's residence, and in the centre are a number of trees.

Got a good mental picture? So, on arrival, we went up to the homestead and enquired as to the possibility of employment but were told by a servant girl that the overseer was away and that we should come back the next day.

That was a disappointment, I don't mind telling you. We were near starving by now, and our hearts and stomachs had anticipated a feed here. Moonlite led us up into the nearby hills in a dark mood. That night, he had an argument with Gus Wernicke, who accused him of cowardice in not taking what he needed from the station.

Moonlite flew into a temper and told him that he was being ungrateful, but Wernicke said that he would have taken us boys and snuck into the property at night and robbed it. As if we boys were his to command. And then I saw Moonlite's rage move to something far worse: 'I'm sending a telegram for your father to collect you at the next town,' he hissed.

We could see Wernicke's knees buckle a little, as if Moonlite had slapped him. For there was only one thing that Wernicke feared – really pissing-yourself bowel-emptying sick-to-the-stomach feared – and that was his father. The old brute had beaten him and abused him in ways we'd never fully know, and, even after he'd run away from him, the fear clearly followed.

And Wernicke, just a moment earlier the big man among us, dropped to a crouch, whimpering like a child, snot bubbling out of his nose as he begged Moonlite not to do it. But it was only the start. Moonlite told him he had a choice: to submit to a thrashing or be returned to his father. Without even pausing to think about it, Wernicke lifted his shirt from his back, where we could see the marks of many previous thrashings.

Nesbitt asked Moonlite not to do it, but he would not be dissuaded. He took a thin branch from a nearby tree and began flailing Wernicke's back until it was a mess of red welts. He finally sat down on the ground, all the anger out of him. And here's the funny thing – young Wernicke took it stoically, not uttering a sound. He might have blubbered at the threat of being returned to his father, but he let us know that, in one thing, he was more experienced and grown up than any of us – taking a beating.

It was a miserable night, and a silence descended over us with the drizzle. It felt to me that there was suddenly an extra, unfamiliar person in camp with us, fracturing our unity. We huddled down, damp, cold and hungry, and tried to get some sleep.

- - -

Recalling his glory days with Garibaldi

The next morning, Moonlite shook us out of our sleeping bags with a renewed vigour. He was wearing his red shirt, as if recalling his glory days with Garibaldi in Italy. Then he led us back down to the station, where he again asked for the overseer but was told we would need to wait for him to finish his meal before seeing us. So we sat and waited. And waited. And waited. All the time, Moonlite's temper was building and his positive demeanour fading. We were kept waiting nearly three hours. We could see Moonlite's face growing grimmer and grimmer as our stomachs rumbled and we shivered from the damp in our clothes.

When Baynes finally appeared, he looked at us as if were boat people or Mormons or something and told us that there was neither work nor hand-outs to be had, and that we should clear off. Moonlite stood up, said nothing, and led us back to our camp once more. He and Gus Wernicke sat up glaring at each other over the fire. It was a more miserable night than the one before. It rained heavily on us until we were shivering like unloved stray dogs left outside in the winter.

Come the next morning, though, Moonlite looked like the rain hadn't touched him. His growing red-hot fury had sizzled it as it neared him. He stood with Gus Wernicke at his side and told us to get our guns ready, proclaiming: 'It is time to take what has been denied us.'

That was the point when everything turned. If we were going to play at being outlaws, we were going to play seriously. Moonlite must have lain awake most of that cold, damp night, fuming over things. The unwillingness of the haves to share with the have-nots. The harsh unwillingness of one man to recognise the basic dignity of another. The ability of the police to harass a man and drive him to this. Social tribalism. Treating the unfortunate as undeserving. The English intolerance of the Irish. The lack of commitment to serious prison reform.

The squattocracy and their self-importance. Government inaction on climate change. Mining magnates who acted like they invented iron ore, rather than being glorified diggers and sellers of dirt and rocks. The expected right of politicians and company executives to be forgiven their thefts and other crimes. The demonisation and the dehumanisation of refugees. The willingness of politicians to play any random race card. Pork-barrelling and cronyism. The extreme ridiculousness of public liability insurance. Moral police. The goldfish attention span of the media. Tacitly sanctioned racial intolerance. Government appropriation and selling of social assets. Welfare cuts.

I mean, when exactly did we become such a mean-spirited nation?

We walked in the back gate of the property, on the afternoon of Saturday 15 November 1879, and Moonlite pointed a pistol at the first servant we saw and told him to bail up. Then we had him lead us inside the farm house. When Baynes saw us, he glared at us as if his eyes could shoot bullets, but Moonlite pressed his gun to his head to keep him in his place.

The first thing he did after securing the property was to get all the guns there and pass them out to us boys. Then he broke open the store room, and we ate our fill. And we were buzzing with the exhilaration of it all. We were singing Queen's *We are the Champions*, in awe of what we were doing. Not really understanding that we should have been singing David Bowie's *We Can be Heroes*. Just for one day!

I'm not sure that Moonlite had thought too much further than that, really. As the day wore on, and several people called to visit, he just added them to our store of prisoners. Mr Weir, the postmaster and storekeeper who we had met a few days previously, was one of the men bailed up, and he gave an interview that was published in the *Argus* on 21 November:

> When I reached the door I heard a noise and looking up I saw that a man had me covered with a gun. From the excited appearance of the man, I said to myself, 'Here is a madman at large', and at once bolted round the house. On getting near the kitchen another man sprang up and confronted me with a revolver. Placing the muzzle of the weapon at my ear, he sang out, 'Bail up'. A third man appeared on the other side, and he also pointed a revolver at my head. Of course I was then obliged to submit, and they marched me into the dining room.

According to Weir, Moonlite accused Baynes of ill-treating him and his gang:

> You turned me out, and would not allow me to stop in an empty hut. I and my mates had therefore to sleep over a cold and rainy night in the ranges. You told us to come back for work, and we did so at the time appointed, but you again ordered us away, as if we were dogs. Now, however, I am master here, and you will have to do as I direct.

He was said to have repeatedly abused Baynes with 'strong language', and things nearly got out of hand when Baynes said to Wernicke, 'Bad work, my boy.' Moonlite went ballistic, accusing Baynes of 'tampering' with the boy. According to the *Argus*, he 'raged like a maniac'.

The station owner himself, Mr Claude McDonald, soon returned with his brother Alexander, who had recently arrived from England. The bushrangers came out to meet them and said, 'Drop your horse, or we will shoot you.' The two men were then taken into the house as well.

Mr McDonald stated that Moonlite caught Baynes by the throat and 'used him roughly, tearing his shirt and swearing that he would drive a bowie-knife into him.' After protests from the other hostages though he suddenly turned on the charm again and let Mr Baynes go. He did take a double-barrelled shotgun from the farm, however, and went out and shot two turkeys in the farmyard and sat down to a very genteel dinner with the McDonald brothers as if he was one of the landed gentry himself.

All the different Moonlites were on display that evening.

- - -

The mock trial

Night fell. Moonlite entertained **us** by subjecting Baynes to a mock trial, threatening to have him hanged for his crimes of injustice towards us. The ladies of the household nearly all fainted away with fear at the thought of this. And Moonlite had to take great pains to assure them that it was all just a threat to keep the brute Baynes in his place. Moonlite actually went out of his way to appear a perfect gentleman with the ladies, entertaining them with tales of his exploits before having us all bed down for the night – men in one room and women in another.

A lesser man might at this point start to wonder what he was getting himself into, but Moonlite was not a lesser man. And none of us wanted to admit that we might be either, regardless of what we were thinking.

The sun seemed to rise earlier the next morning, as if not wanting to miss a moment of the action. As the day wore on, more people called at the house and joined our collection of prisoners.

At 10.30 am, a 16-year-old boy named James Stearman, who had come to deliver the mail, was taken hostage. Shortly after this, Scott rode over to a nearby station to round up the station overseer there. On the way back, he even stopped at the Australian Arms Hotel, bailed up the patrons and escorted them back to the homestead too.

Eventually, we were holding over 35 people. I heard Nesbitt ask Moonlite what he intended to do with all the prisoners, but all he answered was, 'We'll see.'

But I also later heard him ask Nesbitt: 'What do you think the Kellys would do if they were holed up with so many prisoners, just waiting for the police to come and find them?'

'I doubt the Kellys would ever find themselves in this type of situation,' Nesbitt replied – not knowing, of course, that they'd be in an Inn in Glenrowan with a similarly sized party of civilian prisoners, with the police surrounding them, in less than a year.

Now it's worth an aside here to share some wisdom with you about the Kelly gang. Moonlite often told us what they were really like. I mean, they might have memorials and books and statues and all kinds of tourist shit with their pictures on them, but if you took off the metal helmets and really wanted to find out a bit more about who they really were – you'd find a quartet of ignorant bushie bogans. That's what Moonlite reckoned. He went on and on about it all the time. Only one of them could read or write worth shit, they were primary school dropouts with only half an education to share among them. They were thugs who'd be doing over service stations for small change if they could. They'd have collections of empty Jack Daniels bottles all around the front yard and a mongrel three-legged blue heeler, with one eye out, who'd bite anybody who walked past their place. Even the postman who brought them their dole cheque would be savaged. They'd have tats all up and down their arms and dark wraparound mirror sunglasses and noisy motorbikes that they'd strip and reassemble on the lounge room carpet. And they'd play heavy metal music all over the neighbourhood and grow dope in between the tomato plants in the back yard.

If a neighbourhood cat or pet rabbit went missing, its fur might be found in their back yard, ripped apart by their mongrel dog, or hung up on the clothes line for shooting practice. They'd have guns hidden all over the house. Real guns, not air rifles and small calibre pistols. And some nights, they'd get really pissed and sit on the veranda and take a random shot or two at the empty bottles in the yard. If the police ever came to investigate, though, suddenly nobody would be at home, all the lights would be off, and they'd all have alibis about being out drinking with some mate who'd just got out of prison.

If you lived on their street and left your car unlocked overnight, you'd find the stereo gone in the morning – or some half-naked, drug-skinny biker gal would be sleeping in your back seat where she'd been recently rooted, leaving stains on your seat covers. And she'd abuse the fuck at you when you woke her up and wouldn't know shit about your fucking missing stereo and you'd be an arsehole for waking her up, and she'd gather up her things and head back over to the Kelly house where she'd bang on the door screaming like a lunatic for about half an hour but would have no more luck at finding anybody home than the police ever did.

But when the local council guy'd show up to ask them about some problem or complaint, they'd be there. They'd let him inside and all sit around him, fingering tools like hammers and chisels, as if they might be something they'd need to use on their motorbikes just then, until the guy was nearly wetting himself to get back out the door and would just leave his forms and things in their letter box.

And they'd have this big pile of busted TVs and DVD players in the back yard, most of them stolen, attracting snakes and spiders and stuff that would eventually crawl into the neighbours' yards to escape the smell of stale beer and dog shit. And they'd have this shed with padlocks on it like it was the Reserve Bank, that they only went out to late at night. It could have been full of stolen stuff, or drugs or some dead guy being dissolved in a barrel of acid. Who knew?

They were content with life. Content to just take a piss in the front yard whenever it suited them. Content to try to ride their motorbikes past the primary school as stoned as a quarry. Content to not give a fuck what anybody thought of them. Because they were going to be heroes. They were going to be on tea towels and t-shirts and other tourist shit and have historians write endless books about them and have movies made about them starring Heath Ledger. That's what the Kelly gang were like.

At least that's what Captain Moonlite reckoned.

- - -

Back at Wantabadgery station

Anyway, back at Wantabadgery station. As you might have guessed, having so many people abducted from a small community was starting to raise questions. In the middle of the afternoon, a chap named Alexander McDonald had been drinking at Paterson's Hotel and heard that something strange was going on at the station. He rode into Wagga Wagga to alert the police. Another man, Fred Williams, also suspected that something fishy was going on, and he rode to Gundagai to inform the authorities there.

Constable Rowe of Wagga Wagga stated that the news about the Wantabadgery station being bailed up was first reported to him about 7 o'clock on Sunday night. He gathered Constables Headley, John and Williamson, and the four of them set off to investigate, riding through the night.

The story evolved a bit, though. When all the dust and blood had settled, Sub-inspector Medley of Wagga Wagga told the *Argus* that the story he was given on Sunday night was that it was a bunch of drunken shearers at Wantabadgery, which is why he only sent out four constables and didn't go with them himself.

He did, to his credit, not claim that his dog ate the message.

Anyway, the party of four police from Wagga Wagga reached the station about 4 am Monday and waited for dawn before advancing. All they really knew was that local people were going into the main house and then not returning, like it was the Bermuda Triangle. The police left their horses some distance away and tried to sneak up on the house on foot, but a farm dog – not the aforementioned homework-eating dog – started barking and alerted us. Moonlite stepped outside to see what the commotion was about, and seeing the troopers, he opened fire on them.

We were quick to join him, firing like he had taught us. We were pretty bloody

Arrival of the Wagga Police at Wantabadgery Station, by Alfred May and Alfred Martin Ebsworth, *Australasian Sketcher*

terrible shots, I can tell you, but the police didn't know that. After a lucky shot passed through one of the policemen's caps, they quickly turned tail and ran, wading through a small swamp to get away.

We were full of ourselves after that, high fiving each other and whooping like idiots. But Moonlite called us together. It was clearly time to hit the road Jack, and not come back no more, no more, no more, no more. The police would return, full of fury, in the way that we had returned to the station full of fury ourselves, and we'd best be gone when they did.

Moonlite had us mount horses to make our escape. But let me tell you, when a horse knows that you don't know how to ride, it doesn't cut you any slack. In fact, it goes out of its way to be contrary and make you look like a dickhead on a saddle. So the only road we hit for some time was when one of us fell off his horse. As a result, it took us quite a while to get any distance away. Also, we kept encountering people, because men had started coming in from all directions to find out what was happening or to help out.

John Beveridge, who had been one of the hostages, rode straight home to round up men and guns. A dozen armed men organised by the contractors Fishburn and Morton, who were constructing the Junee to Narrandera railway, joined in. And Senior Sergeant Carroll came from Gundagai with four constables, and another policeman, Constable Wyles, came from Bethungra.

As we travelled along, we met up with Beveridge's armed party. However, their courage failed them when Moonlite bailed them up. He took their weapons and made them stand in a line – along with a party of six shearers who had come along. Moonlite was full of rage that these men were clearly intent on hunting him down, and he announced that he intended to put Beveridge and his two 'accomplices' on trial. A jury was formed by the roadside from the shearers, but they found the men 'not guilty'. This infuriated Moonlite further, and he executed one of the horses instead. He then sentenced the men to kneel down and he walked down the line and kicked each of them.

We headed off again but soon met the aforementioned Constable Wyles from Bethungra. We disarmed him too and forced him to accompany us to the farm house of Mr McGlede. Remember them? I am sorry that we chose to repay their former kindness with a visit. Only Mrs McGlede was home, and Moonlite was quick to assure her that we meant no harm. We partook of milk and brandy before preparing to leave.

- - -

Things beyond our view were now happening at a very rapid pace.

As the police searched for the bushrangers, the news was way ahead of them. A telegram from Wagga Wagga, reported in several newspapers, stated that ten men had stuck up Wantabadgery station. This was later downgraded to seven armed men, before being reduced again to six – although it was suspected that one of them was Dan Kelly! (Yeah, I know, I know.)

Telegrams went to all the towns in the region. Special constables were called out and police told to get their butts and their gun-butts ready and into action. As bushranger hysteria set in, special constables placed the town of Gundagai under guard. In Wagga, the banks had staff arm themselves.

The *Sydney Morning Herald* reported that the bushrangers were keeping 'a large part of the Lachlan and Murrumbidgee district in a state of terror'. If we could have watched this unfolding on TV, like the OJ Simpson car chase, we would have been gobsmacked at what others were making of it all.

A quick word on McGlede's hut might come in handy about here. That *Argus* wannabe home renovation writer later described it as being built of slabs and consisting of four rooms and a separate kitchen building. For a bit of colour, the writer added that it also had a nice fruit garden in front.

I didn't pay too much attention to the garden, in truth, because we were just heading back to the road when the police came into view.

The shit had come home to roost. The chickens had hit the fan.

Another irony moment here. If we'd really been the bad-arse bushrangers that the police had come gunning for, we'd have been long since gone-baby-gone, with only our dust left behind. I reckon, if we'd been walking, we'd have gotten further away.

- - -

To be honest, the order of events that followed was a little bit confusing

Even to those of us who were there, the many conflicting reports didn't make it much easier to figure things out afterwards. But here's what I can tell you – we saw the police approaching and panicked. We could even see armed civilians appearing on the hills around us, coming to join in the fray. Moonlite told us to stand and fight. Constable Wyles ran for his life and joined up with the police. We took cover behind fences and trees or back inside the McGlede's place. Then Moonlite ordered us all into the hut to prepare our guns.

According to the *Australasian Sketcher* report, Constable Gorman was the closest to the bushrangers. He called out, 'Surrender!' but the bushrangers replied, 'No, come on and fight, you ____, come on and fight: no surrender!' I've never recalled what word so offended the reporter that he was unable to write it – leaving it to everyone's imagination. For all I know it could have been fuckitty-douchebag-dickwit-prick-brained-arseandtitlickers. Or maybe not. Insert what word you think would be appropriate.

At that point, both sides started shooting like ____ crazy people.

It took us a few moments to realise that Gus Wernicke wasn't with us. We looked out the windows and saw him out in the yard beside a fence post, blazing away at the police as if each of them was his father. He held the police back as he moved from fence to log, his face set in grim determination.

It was marvellous to see. But then his gun ran empty. As he bent down to reload it, one of the policemen stood up, took careful aim and shot him. Wernicke grunted and fell to the ground, his blood and his life seeping out of him and into the dry earth beneath.

Time slowed then. Nesbitt had been trying to stop Moonlite from stepping out to join Wernicke, but now his hands fell away. Moonlite lifted his rifle and stepped outside the hut, completely fearless, like a man made of iron.

The police all now turned their guns towards Moonlite, and so did all those armed lunatics on the hills around us. Dozens of guns fired at him, but he didn't flinch. He fired, stepped forward, fired again, stepped forward, fired again. He was going to march right up to the police lines like this, but then he turned his head and looked at the body of Gus Wernicke, now being clubbed viciously by a trooper. Moonlite lifted his gun, pointed it at the closest policeman, Constable Bowen-Webb, and fired. The policeman fell like a calf that had had a shotgun discharged against its forehead.

The police went crazy then. Of course. He was a Cop-Killer! They opened up on Moonlite like a SWAT team with automatic weapons. Even Moonlite had to step back now. He re-entered the hut, but the fusillade of bullets followed him. He brought the police fury down on top of us like – well, like a police fury coming down on top of us!

You know how it looks in the movies, when a sustained hail of heavy-calibre machine gun fire rips a house or shack to pieces, with splinters and glass flying all over and shelves falling down and ceiling lights dropping. It was like that. I was hit in the arm and fell back into the chimney hearth for shelter, and Nesbitt was also hit – a single bullet struck him in the temple.

He staggered and fell, and Moonlite's defiance and anger and fury and rage fell with him. He let go of his gun and dropped down beside James Nesbitt, cradling his head in his hands, tears falling into his dark hair. His fight was over. His purpose for fighting now gone.

'Oh my poor boy. My poor boy,' he said. 'What have they done to you?'

But that wasn't the real question, was it. It should have been: 'What have I done to you?'

The police were kicking in the doors and climbing in the windows now. They forced us all to the ground and tied our arms tightly behind our backs. I had a bullet wound in the arm, but they didn't care. They had us. Well, all of us except for Thomas Rogan. His bravado had fled at the first shots. He hid under the bed in the bedroom and wasn't found until the next morning. The rest of us were led out with our jackets over our heads like we were hiding from the glare of flashing police car sirens and bright camera lights, stumbling around, not knowing what would come next.

Now one thing about gunshot wounds – despite them hurting like all buggery – they rarely kill you straight away. They cause a horrible mess of your flesh and stuff, and blood and life just sort of ebbs out of you, and you slip slowly into the chill grip of death. Or maybe we were just made of sterner stuff back then than all those movie German soldiers and baddie spies and anybody at all who goes up against Bruce Willis – who die immediately from the smallest of pistol wounds.

Well, Gus Wernicke slipped into death's grasp at about 3 o'clock. James Nesbitt followed two hours later. Senior Constable Bowen-Webb was transported to Gundagai by wagon, and despite all efforts to save him, he too died, six days later on Sunday 23 November.

- - -

Variations on a theme

In trying to find some order to the chaotic events, and interviewing only the police, the media came up with several variations on the story.

One of the policemen, Constable Barry, stated in an interview run in the *Argus* that his horse was shot out from under him as he approached the hut. He was shot at again, looked around and saw Gus Wernicke shooting at him. 'He was in fact more full of fight than any other member of the gang,' he was reported to have said.

Barry then returned fire and shot Wernicke. 'He staggered, and fell upon his left side. The bullet had pierced his body, entering at the side and coming out at the spine.'

The *Australasian Sketcher*, however, credited Constable Bowen-Webb with shooting both Wernicke and Nesbitt before being shot himself – all 'witnessed by a large number of persons, who looked on from hills in the vicinity'.

The *Argus* stated, of Wernicke's death: 'It has not been ascertained by whom the fatal shot was fired.' Constable Rowe of Wagga Wagga put in a claim to have shot Nesbitt, but the *Argus* reported: 'Constable Gorman had in the meantime got inside the residence, and, firing through the back window, shot one of the bushrangers dead.'

In another article, though, it stated:

> One of the bushrangers in the house begged of Moonlite to cease firing, or they would all be shot. He threw his arms round Moonlite to pull him back, and as he did so he was shot dead by Constable Bowen-Webb.

The way the *Argus* related Bowen-Webb's shooting:

> After the boy fell, Constable Bowen-Webb advanced to the spot. While in the act of stooping down to load his rifle he was fired upon. The ball took effect, entering the neck, and passed down the back.

Constable Rowe said:

> Quite a scene occurred when Moonlite was brought in and saw his trustiest mate with the death wound on his forehead. Falling upon his form, he kissed him and affectionately wept over him and cried, 'Will he really die? Oh, he is my only dear friend; but for him a great many more lives would have been lost.'

The police wanted the bushrangers to identify themselves and got the names Andrew Scott, Graham Bennett and Thomas Williams. No one would give the name of the two dead youths and, after taking a head count, the police realised that one was missing. The *Argus* told it like this:

> It being known that the gang was composed of six men, and five only being accounted for, a search was immediately made for the missing man. No traces of him, however, could be found, and it was supposed that he had escaped on horseback. Three of the police went in pursuit, but without success.

Of course they had no success. We were all kept under guard at the hut while they searched for him, and the *Argus* told well what happened next:

> In the morning Mr McGlede informed Sergeant Cassin that he had discovered that a man was concealed under his bed, and he believed him to be the missing bushranger. A rush of policemen was at once made and the man was dragged out.

So they had us all. Both dead and alive.

- - -

The cold bare cells in Gundagai

In shock and silence, we were taken to the holding cells in Gundagai. They are bare, chill cells, cold even in November. The dark thick rock holds the misery of all those who had been in them before us.

Moonlite, with more experience of this than any of us, explained that there would be an initial hearing. This would be our chance to tell our side of the story, and even the newspapers would have to listen to us. He was only partially right in that as the newspapers seemed more interested in writing their own stories than his.

Moonlite conducted his own defence with 'insolence towards the bench' and 'great bravado'. He claimed that he and his men had never aimed at the police, only at their horses, and that one of the policemen had clearly shot Constable Bowen-Webb.

No one bought that. Rather, the newspapers quoted the police, proposing that the motivation for Moonlite's actions was 'his burning desire for notoriety' which had 'driven him to make an attempt to outshine the Kellys'.

The *Australasian Sketcher* agreed:

> Truly, the success of the Kelly gang, who have now evaded capture for over 12 months, is having a very encouraging effect on the criminal class.

By Wednesday 19 November, several Victorian police had arrived at Gundagai to identify the prisoners and dead men. And do you know what the local papers printed? They said: 'The Melbourne police have arrived and identified one man as Augustus Wrenckel, son of a publican in Swanston-street.' And then: 'They also identify Nesbitt and Moonlite; but there are none of the Kellys.'

None of the Kellys! Like it is such a disappointment.

But we're not going to talk about the Kellys, right?

The newspapers also ran a constant series of updates on the state of the rapidly deteriorating Constable Bowen-Webb:

> Constable Bowen-Webb is rapidly sinking and is considered past recovery.

and:

> Constable Bowen-Webb is in a very critical condition.

Of course, they soon reported that he was dead. The charges against us suddenly ramped up in seriousness. And then Moonlite changed his tune a little, stating that he would be willing to be hanged, if only the lives of 'his boys' could be saved.

You had to love him for that.

- - -

A couple of other facts

There were a couple of other facts some astute journalists successfully discovered. One reporter wrote of Thomas Rogan that he had every reason:

> to believe that this prisoner, who is about 26, and the oldest of the three, has given an assumed name, and that he has a respectable mother and married sister residing in Melbourne.

There – the truth was out. There was no Rogan. His name was Brown, a fact he'd successfully kept from the police and courts and lawyers and also from us. But as for more juicy facts, such as whether Moonlite actually robbed the bank at Mount Egerton, or had a hand in it, and who shot Constable Bowen-Webb, sorry, you won't get confirmation of that. No, not today. Come back and check this site tomorrow and see whether it has been updated. Or maybe in a few weeks. Perhaps you'll even recall that you read the answer to those questions somewhere, and wake up in the dead of night and spend several hours searching through this text to find it.

Well, good luck. I've been on that journey many times myself.

- - -

Capture of Moonlite and his gang, *The Illustrated Australian News*

Found guilty

We were found guilty in short order in the hearing and all transported to Sydney to stand trial for murder. And so the story now risks becoming one of those courtroom dramas, which drag on and on and on and on. And on. But bear with me a bit – you've made this much of the journey, and there's not too much more to tell – just a few revelations.

When we walked into the court in Sydney, the judge gave us all the evil eye – like we were a pack of bogan, backwards-sunglasses-wearing, singleted, tattooed, dick-headed yobbos who were there on a charge of king-hitting a young kid outside a pub and putting him into a coma. Perhaps we were the equivalent of that at the time. He was Judge Windeyer. Remember that name? The former owner of Wantabadgery station was also a Windeyer. Yep – his brother.

The trial lasted four days, from Monday 8 December though to Thursday 11 December 1879, in the Central Criminal Court of Sydney. Mr J. Want, instructed by Mr H. Smith, defended us lads, but Scott chose to defend himself.

The best coverage of the trial was through the lengthy reporting in the *Sydney Morning Herald,* which did something you don't see often in the media, for the journalist reported Moonlite's criticisms of the way the press had already judged him and the gang. But that was a rarity. Not only were there letters and articles getting stuck into us each day, when we were being transported to Sydney from Gundagai, the stations along the way were crowded with men hooting and crying for our blood.

Of Moonlite's claim against his character assassinations, the *Sydney Morning Herald* article said:

> He had read a number of extracts from papers, and had seen a career painted for him in them which was utterly false. It was alleged that

he had been charged with a variety of crimes, and such a number of insinuations had been thrown out against him that he thought it was only in that dock that he had a chance of answering them.

Moonlite also used the trial as a platform to complain about writers throwing dirt at him because of his very special relationship with Nesbitt. And when he told a journalist that Nesbitt's spirit had frequently appeared to him in his cell, the journalist wrote: 'But I fancy that the 'manifestation' was owing to his having been told that the judge who was to try him is a confirmed spiritualist'.

Not every journalist had him in their sights though. One reporter wrote:

> He impressed me, I must confess. I first met him in Melbourne soon after he was released from Pentridge Gaol, where he served some seven years (out of ten) for the robbery of the Egerton Bank.

More typical, however, was this report:

> He is a madman; that is, so far as all those who think deeply on one subject are so. He has what I should call strong homicidal impulses. Whenever he lectured he invariably carried firearms, and was fond of levelling them at imaginary objects. As a lecturer Scott was fervent, and though the judge who tried him said he had only a veneer of education his order of intellect is by no means of the common.

We were charged with the murder of Constable Bowen-Webb, but not of bailing up or robbery of the Wantabadgery station, so most of the statements and examinations centred on two central things: who shot Bowen-Webb, and what type of gun shot him?

The judge told the jury that, in cases where witnesses were very 'excited' (as was the case here), 'the jury would find contradictions or discrepancies were certain to occur where people told the truth', and if everybody told the same story, they were more likely to have been concocted.

I like that paradox. The more varied and contradictory stories are, the more likely they are to be true!

Anyway, Moonlite's questions and statements to the court were rather long-winded and circuitous, it must be admitted. When he evoked laughter from the court, the judge actually threatened that 'if there were any indecent laughter in the Court, the person so offending would be immediately apprehended and brought before him'.

The police, true to the judge's opinion on the truth, gave contradictory accounts. The only thing they easily agreed on was that Moonlite had shot Constable Bowen-Webb. Until the firearms expert gave his testimony.

You see, the police at first stated that Constable Bowen-Webb was killed by a Snyder rifle, which Scott was shooting with. But a gun-maker called to give testimony, stated that the bullet retrieved from Bowen-Webb's body was a pistol bullet that fitted a Colt revolver. The prosecution then turned to the question of who did have Colt revolvers, and a police witness stated that he observed Williams and I had such guns.

Senior Sergeant Carroll stated that he had recovered two Colt revolvers, and one of them had fired two shots. But he said he believed that one was taken from myself or Thomas Williams. Constable Wyles said that I ran out of the house with a revolver in my hand, and he arrested me. Scott said that I was inside the house, wounded, and was not in possession of any weapons. Scott also said that I could not fire a pistol well, because of my wounds. Constable Gorman said that he arrested me in the kitchen. Mrs McGlede, who was inside the kitchen with us, said that she did not see me or Williams fire a pistol. And Moonlite declared it most likely that one of the other policemen or one of the civilians who were taking pot shots at us from the distance shot Bowen-Webb.

The judge cut through all that, telling the jury that it was not necessary to show which particular prisoner shot Bowen-Webb, according to reports:

> If the jury believed the evidence that Bowen-Webb was shot by any of them they were entitled to find that all the prisoners were acting together, and that Bowen-Webb died in consequence.

Bugger!

- - - -

Like a courtroom drama

Moonlite's discourses and cross-examinations were so longwinded, going on and on and on and on like a courtroom drama, that one of the jury actually complained about it:

> It was the wish of the jury that his Honour should keep Scott within reasonable limits in conducting his examination, and not allow him to drift in irrelevant matters, as he had been doing nearly all through the case.

But Moonlite finally had the stage and was not going to be denied it. He gave a long outline of his life since arriving in New South Wales and Victoria, telling how he had been ill-treated and persecuted and denied an ability to make his way in life honestly. He also told everyone that he was committed to the asylum in Maitland not as a result of being mad or feigning madness, but because he had been drinking heavily before being arrested and 'not getting any stimulants in Maitland he was considered to be mad'.

He was charged with many crimes he did not commit, he stated, including the murder of an actor named Bates, the robbery of the Lancefield bank and freeing prisoners. He committed none of these. And he believed that the police were persecuting him for seeking to uncover the injustices being perpetrated inside Pentridge.

He gave the police a serve, saying: 'Some constables had fought well, but there were others who had fought not but lied well.' Also:

> If the jury would look carefully through the case and examine the

evidence for the prosecution they would find that the case for the Crown was a piece of patchwork.

Then he turned to the jury and sought mercy for us. He did a fine job of it too, I'll grant him that. He declared that we were young and 'not fit food for the gallows'.

Then he passed judgment on the testimony of each of the witnesses as if he was the judge and not a prisoner. Unfortunately, at the end of his lengthy discourse, the lawyer Mr Want did not jump to his feet and applaud, tears streaming from his eyes. Instead, Want advised the jury that they should forget what Moonlite had said, as it was not in his best interests, nor that of us boys. His line of defence was, the *Sydney Morning Herald* reported:

> They were in company of Scott when the latter committed a murder, but it was not shown that they were consenting parties, and, therefore, they could not be held to be guilty of the murder.

Finally, after several days of back and forward testimony, it was time for the judge to sum up. He rolled up his sleeves – metaphorically – and proved that he could be just as boring and repetitious as Moonlite had been. He all but directed the jury the find us all guilty, telling them several times that they only had to be convinced that one of us shot Constable Bowen-Webb for us all to be guilty. He went on to state that only the bushrangers had the type of pistols that the fatal bullet came from anyway. He even went so far as to name the man he thought had fired the fatal shot. The report of his speech, relating to the pistol in question, stated:

> It appeared to be the only weapon that was likely to have killed Bowen-Webb. There was blood upon it. How did that blood come upon it? Bennett was wounded… There were only two persons in the kitchen from whom blood could have come. Nesbitt was shot in the temple, and the jury would have to consider whether Nesbitt would be likely to handle revolvers after he was shot, or whether the evidence did not show beyond any doubt as to the fact that this revolver was found upon this prisoner.

He was pointing at me. Graham Bennett. Naïve young lad led astray. Introduced to violence and lawlessness. Had a gun put into his hands. But pulled the trigger himself.

One other thing I should perhaps mention – because, if I don't, somebody else will dig it up one day. A one-time confidant of Moonlite, Mr Thatcher, visited him in prison and talked to the other lads. Later, he was reported to have stated: 'amongst themselves it is known that Bennett fired the fatal shot.'

But I hope you don't expect me to confirm that, do you?

- - - -

What Moonlite never did

To be completely fair to the mass media of the time, while they accused Moonlite of many reprehensible acts, it is worth pointing out for the record that there were some things they didn't accuse him of. These included: stealing over five thousand pounds from the steamer *Avoca*, between Sydney and Melbourne in 1877. The Eugowra goldfield robbery of 1862. Betrayal of Ben Hall to the police in 1865. The shipwreck of the *Loch Ard*, which sank off the Victorian coast in 1878 with a loss of all hands except two. The Lambing Flats anti-Chinese riots of 1861. The disappearance of Ludwig Leichhardt in central Australia. The cricket riot of February 1879, when 200 spectators mobbed the pitch in Sydney and attacked the visiting English team after a poor decision by the umpire. The start of the Zulu wars in South Africa. The loss of Burke and Wills in central Australia in 1861. Triggering the Eureka Stockade rebellion. The death of Truganini in Tasmania in 1876. The assassination attempt on Prince Alfred, son of Queen Victoria, in Sydney in 1868. Causing the severe drought of 1865–1869. Advising the Victorian Acclimatisation Society on the introduction of rabbits, foxes and blackberries to Australia. Convincing the Australian colonies to have different gauge rail tracks. Henry Parkes' sense of beardliness. The shipwreck of the *Princess Alice*, which collided with the steam collier *Bywell Castle* in the Thames River in 1878 and sank, killing at least 600. The great Chicago fire of 1871. Karl Marx's *Communist Manifesto*. Terrorism. Zionism. Jingoism. Fascism. Apologism. Postmodernism. The US occupation of the Philippines. The Great Train Robbery of Nevada in 1870. The more than 100-year-long Chinese Taiping Rebellion. Convincing the deposed Napoleon Bonaparte to escape from the island of Elba in the Mediterranean and re-establish himself as emperor of France. The assassination of King Umberto I of Italy. The murder of Wild Bill Hickok while playing cards. The Boxer

Rebellion in China. The assassination of Archduke Franz Ferdinand in Sarajevo that triggered World War One. The Dreyfus Affair in France. Every stupid military decision made by General Haig. The disappearance of Prime Minister Harold Holt while swimming at Portsea. Introducing Elvis Presley to hamburgers. Convincing Michael Jackson he'd look better with whiter skin. Selling Buddy Holly his plane ticket. The Exxon-Valdez oil spill in Alaska. French nuclear testing in the Pacific. The Bhopal Union Carbide chemical disaster. The fashion of sideburns and flared trousers. Disco music. Leg warmers. The axing of the series *Deadwood* and *Firefly*. The never-ending of the series *Lost*. The murder of John Lennon. Teaching Vice President Dick Cheney how to shoot. Wearing socks and sandals. Mullet haircuts. Safari suits. Boob tubes. Mirrored sunglasses. Stars of the southern cross tattoos on the necks of yobbos. The government's policies on boat people. One Nation. Selling ownership of Vegemite to Americans. Anti-vaccination theories. Global climate change denial. Animal onesies. Islamic State. Donald Trump's presidency. Covid-19. Google specs and Fox News.

I think that needed to be stated, that the media never accused him of any of those things, as I said, just to be fair.

- - -

Meanwhile, back in the court room

So, back in the court room, we were sweating it out, waiting for those 12 good citizens of the jury to decide whether we were to live or die. And I can tell you that we suddenly understood that we were very mortal. The fact that we might die on the decision of these men suddenly defined everything to us. We were worth nothing more than a random vote. Those long minutes of waiting were all that existed. Such long, long minutes, and that awareness of death made life so much more precious that we prayed desperately to cling to it just a little longer. Even if it was in listening to the judge out-Moonlite Moonlite in his ramblings.

An aside here: if you really want to reform the jury system, you should get 12 people and sit them down at a dinner party. Put them in their comfort zone, rather than in a strange room in an official building. They could have a good feed and a few drinks and really go to town telling each other what they thought of every problem in the nation and the world, and what ought to be done to fix them. They could parrot popular slogans and Facebook facts and evidence based on a sample size of one at each other, so you'd not only get a judgment on whether the defendants were guilty or not, but you'd get policy ideas for health care reform, education improvements, restorative justice, peace in the Middle East, Aboriginal advancement – you name it. And you wouldn't even have to develop a system to support and fund it! These types of juries are operating across the country every weekend of the year.

But back to the coverage of our trial:

> The jury returned into Court at precisely 6 o'clock, having been in consultation for two hours and seven minutes, and returned a verdict of 'GUILTY' against all four prisoners, but recommended Rogan, Williams and Bennett to mercy.

Moonlite at once took to his feet. This was his chance to go down in history with a popular sound bite. He could have done something like Ned Kelly's response to Judge Redmond Barry after being sentenced to death, standing there like a belligerent bearded hipster barista, saying, 'I will go a little further than that, and say I will see you there when I go'. But he didn't. Moonlite was off again.

He said, in part, according to the *Sydney Morning Herald* report:

> He was aware that his Honour would do his duty and sentence him to death, and standing there as he did with the warm blood pouring through every vein in his body, he was to be sentenced to death; and he knew it was coming and did not fear it.

That wasn't too bad, but then he went on and on about witnesses perjuring themselves and said he would go to his fate on the scaffold and would be a happier man than any of those who went into the witness box and swore a lie.

Then he gave the jury a bit of a serve, which was reported as him stating:

> Almighty God, who judged us all by the broad page of His life, and he believed that God would show him more mercy than his fellow men would show him; and he could look forward with hope beyond the grave and stand on the gallows without one trembling limb and meet his fate.

His final words before sitting down were:

> If the law has been so broken that it must be avenged by a human life let me be the victim and spare these youths. God created them for something better than the gallows.

- - - -

The judge gave Moonlite both barrels

When he was done, the judge gave him both barrels at close quarters, throwing in all of his own thoughts and personal judgments that he could not by rights have expressed during the case, like the 'bad guy' judge on Colonial Australia's Got Talent. He said:

> Your whole career is marked by conduct as outrageous and as horrible as ever disgraced any band of bushrangers in this country...the victim of your murder shot down by you when in the execution of his duty will live in the memory of all who admire devotion to the cause of duty and manliness, whilst your fate will only give an additional warning to the reckless criminal that the way of transgressors is hard, and that a felon's death and an ignominious grave await those who commence a career of crime!

So wound up was he that the *Sydney Morning Herald* reporter noted:

> During the remarks made by his Honour when passing sentence, he was more than once overcome by emotion, in consequence of which it was at times difficult to hear all that he said.

Moonlite finally came up with a coherent response, much later, writing in his gaol cell:

> We had no intention of being bushrangers, every fact supports me, every thing speaks to the broad truth that misery and hunger

produced despair and in one wild hour we proved how much the wretched dare. It must be seen that Wantabadgery was the place where the voice of hunger drowned the voice of reason, and we became criminals.

- - - -

So how much of a bad-ass bushranger was Moonlite really in the big scheme of things?

Moonlite had endless hysterical press coverage after the Wantabadgery shootings, so you'd easily think he was some kind of grand robber and mass murderer. But just one single policeman was shot dead – and that might not even have been by Moonlite. Just one!

The Kelly gang were right up the top of the bad-ass bushranger list, of course. They'd been much more successful at bank robbing and had shot three policemen dead at Stringybark Creek. They also shot Aaron Sherritt, their former gang supporter, when they suspected him of treason. They wounded a few more police at their final shoot-out at Glenrowan too – but it was as much the theatre of that which stuck in the public's imagination.

Who else was there? Let's test your knowledge of bushrangers.

Well, Ben Hall must have been right up there as a bad-ass bushranger, right? You probably know him as a romantic bushranger, for some reason you're not sure of. Maybe there was a folk song written about him, meaning that he had to be more good than bad, wronged by the system and loved by a woman. Or maybe he was just more clean shaven than some of the other bushrangers. He'd robbed quite a few stagecoaches, but in fact he hadn't killed anyone when police surrounded him and shot him dead near Forbes in New South Wales in 1865.

Okay, what about Frank Gardiner, who was linked with Ben Hall? He must have been quite a bad-ass, shoot 'em up bushranger. There's something about his name that sounds dangerous even, and you might have an image of a man with black moustache and beard. He tried very hard to be a killer. He wounded five policemen, but he didn't manage to kill anyone either.

What about Captain Thunderbolt or that Wild Colonial Boy, Jack Donahue? How did they rate on the list of bad-ass bushrangers? Here are the statistics:

I Maurice S. O'Connor being the Medical Officer of the Gaol at Darlinghurst do hereby declare and certify that I have this day witnessed the execution of Andrew George Scott alias Moonlight lately convicted and duly sentenced to death at the Supreme Criminal Court Sydney and I further certify that the said Andrew George Scott alias Moonlight was in pursuance of such sentence hanged by the neck until his body was dead.

Given under my hand this twentieth day of January in the year 1880

Maurice S. O'Connor
Visiting Surgeon

J.W. Rotherston
Ch. Sd.
20.1.80

We the undersigned do hereby declare and testify that we have this day been present when the extreme penalty of the Law was executed on the body of Andrew George Scott alias Moonlight lately convicted at the Supreme Criminal Court Sydney held on the Eleventh day of December 1879 and duly sentenced to death and that the said Andrew George Scott alias Moonlight was in pursuance of said sentence hanged by the neck until his body was dead.

Charles Cowper — Sheriff
T. Thurlow — Under Sheriff
[signature] — Principal Gaoler
J. Mansfield — Visiting Magistrate
Michl Burke — Chief Warder
[signature] Inspector General of Police
Wm Maguire [illegible]

Henry Mickle — Coroner
Louis C. Joskel L.R.C.P.
Mr [illegible]
Peter Miller J.P.
Ernest Carter J.P.
John Stewart
Daniel O'Connor
[signatures]

Darlinghurst Gaol
Signed 20 January 1880

Ben Hall killed no one. Frank Gardiner wounded a policeman, but never killed anyone. Captain Starlight killed no one. Martin Cash killed one person.

So who actually killed more people than Moonlite did? There was Mad Dog Morgan, who roamed around the Murray River. He shot and killed three policemen. Police finally gunned him down in Victoria in 1865, souveniring his head for examination and his scrotum to make a tobacco pouch. For just three!

The Clarke brothers, who ranged around Queanbeyan and the South Coast of New South Wales, like early day rogue public servants from Canberra on holidays, were said to have killed five policemen and committed 36 holdups before being captured and hanged in 1867. But have you heard of them? They are often listed as the most deadly bushrangers in Australia, and you probably don't know anything about them.

The US Wild West gunfighters, by comparison, really knew how to mark up notches on their pistols. The top league bad-ass gunfighter was John Wesley Harden, the psychopath son of a Methodist preacher, credited with 42 killings. Next in line – or perhaps number one on the list, depending on how you count – is Tom Horn, credited with 50 killings, though about half of them were during his time as a rather violent and trigger-happy lawman before he was dismissed and became a hired gun.

Jim Miller, known affectionately as 'Killer Miller', is thought to have killed between 14 and 50 people. After his arrest in 1909, the townspeople of Ada, Oklahoma, broke into his cell, dragged him to a local barn and lynched him.

Billy the Kid is said to have killed up to 21 people, described as one for every year of his life. But in fact, it might have been as low as five. And Jesse James, one of the most famous of gunslingers and robbers, is believed to have killed 12 people, including a young girl – not counting those he killed in the Civil War.

What is my point? Well, clearly in the USA, the deadly measure of a gunslinger had something to do with the number of people he'd killed. In Australia, it was something else that brought you fame. Sure, waving guns around during a robbery made you dangerous, but actual killing was much rarer. There are theories that the Wild West was much bloodier than the Australian outback because the American Civil War, which raged from 1861 to 1865, left over 600,000 men dead. So shooting one or two people dead hardly compared to that carnage.

Moonlite saw his replacement in the public's imagination by all the other, more famous, bushrangers as another injustice. Despite the amount of hysteria around his capture and trial, he lacked the theatre of the Kellys (they really did have a good agent!) and the more traditional clean-shaven romance of Ben Hall. Or maybe it was the gay thing?

I mean, who can really tell, at the time, what is going to mark a person as memorable in history and what isn't? The Clarke brothers will tell you that it wasn't for lack of trying that they slipped out of the public imagination. Maybe it takes a telemovie and bestselling book? Or a tourist stop full of memorabilia? I don't know for sure, but I do know that it takes more than an eccentric and unstable middle-aged man with a gang of young boys walking around remote New South Wales, engaging in petty larceny and killing only one policeman.

- - - -

Scott and Rogan's Execution, *The Bulletin*

Moonlite's last days

Moonlite spent his few remaining days in his death cell, writing long and meandering letters. In the montage ending of the movie, you'd see him sitting there in the dark with this solemn music playing in the background. Perhaps there'd be flashbacks to the main story, even showing some intimate moments between him and Nesbitt, or maybe even showing who really shot Bowen-Webb. Maybe.

But there is no montage in real life. The days and hours and minutes and seconds just tick past slowly. And Moonlite filled that painful time by retelling his life, arguing that he was innocent of everything that he had been accused of – the Mount Egerton robbery, passing bad cheques in Sydney, all the crimes that he was accused of that he never committed, and the Wantabadgery shoot-out. Particularly the Wantabadgery shoot-out! He dwelt on that over and over, explaining how he couldn't have shot Constable Bowen-Webb. Explaining that the shooting was the culmination of all the wrongs that had been aligned against him. All the injustices that prevented him from living the good life that he would surely otherwise have lived. Surely!

He'd such an intellect and imagination, and I sometimes imagine the things he could have written, knowing that his time was ending, with the solitude and the focus he had. He could have told our story of living in Fiji. He could have resurrected each of us and created a different life for us. But he just kept on about the same old things. That was the final disappointment for us boys. Worse than dying and being imprisoned. For we'd always expected that, but he'd taught us to dream of something else.

He was also said to have written a confession, which he handed to one Canon Rich, but it has never been found. And his final request, repeated many times, was simply to be buried near his beloved James Nesbitt. In one letter, he wrote:

> I am to die on the 20th instant, and hope that I may rest with my friend. The only thing I long for is the certainty that I may share his grave.

He wrote to Nesbitt's mother of her son – perhaps with a little more information than a late 19th century mother who had just lost her son wanted to know about their relationship:

> his hopes were my hopes his grave will be my resting place and I trust I may be worthy to be with him when we shall all meet to part no more, when an all-seeing God who can read all hearts will be the judge long before I am with him and in his grave.

It didn't really matter what she might have thought of that, though, since none of his death cell letters were ever delivered. The authorities stuck them in a box to gather dust for a century.

- - - -

In late January 1880, Moonlite's erratic and fanciful and reimagined life finally came to its end

So the day finally came when Moonlite and Rogan were led to the scaffold at the Darlinghurst Gaol. He wore on his finger a ring woven from Nesbitt's hair. And, according to the *Brisbane Courier* of Wednesday 21 January 1880:

> Rogan was stolid and apparently indifferent. When the white caps had been drawn over the faces of the two men, they shook hands with each other. Immediately afterwards the bolt was drawn. Scott died instantaneously, but Rogan struggled convulsively for a few minutes. The gaol surgeon, however, considered that both were insensible from the moment they fell.

The doctor officially declared the two men bereft of life. Moonlite's metabolic processes ended. He'd fallen off the twig. Kicked the bucket. Shuffled off this mortal coil. Run down the curtains and joined the bleedin' choir invisible. He was an ex-parrot!

Or, as I'd like to imagine, he journeyed on to that undiscovered country from whose bourn no traveller returns – somewhere something like Fiji.

Or perhaps we could just say he was history!

As for the last pair of us, myself and Williams, following two appeals against our sentences, the Executive Council commuted our sentences to life imprisonment. But Williams would only live five more years, being hanged for the stabbing of a fellow inmate inside Berrima Goal.

And me? If you search, you'll find that the best conjecture says that my fate remains a mystery. It has been assumed that I served my time, or may have died in prison, but that 'hopefully, one day what happened to him will be discovered, and another chapter in the annals of bushranging history will be complete.'

Yeah, right.

- - - -

Moonlite's grave in Gundagai cemetery "A rough, unhewn rock, one that skilled hands could have made into something better."

What else should I tell you?

Or what else should I hide from you? Perhaps the story about Ned Kelly's remains and Moonlite's remains. One last comparison between the two men. Ned Kelly was hanged later that same year, in November 1880, and was buried in the cemetery at the Old Melbourne Gaol. When the prison yard was excavated in 1929, there was a general scramble to souvenir his bones. The *Argus* described it:

> The edge of the shovel ripped off the lid of the coffin, which was made of redgum, and a skeleton was revealed. As soon as this gruesome discovery was made, a crowd of young boys who had been standing round expectantly while eating their luncheons rushed forward and seized the bones. The workmen intervened, but in the scramble portions of the skeleton were carried off, including even the teeth.

His remains, and those of the other prisoners from the gaol, were moved to Pentridge Prison, and over time their exact locations were lost. Fast forward to 2002, when excavation work at Pentridge to develop apartments found a body. So, suddenly, there was this big fuss about finding all those prisoners' remains – in particular, finding Ned Kelly. People were excavating sites looking for his body as if it was a Roman Treasure, rather than the bones of a bogan bushranger. After a long and sustained search, both in the archives and in the dirt, 21 coffins were found. And one of them had to be Ned's. That, in turn, led to a long scientific search to identify Kelly's bones and to find his skull. They finally found him, and the story made the front pages of the papers. It even made headlines overseas.

The long and the short of that story was that his remains were returned to his family and buried in an unmarked grave at Greta, near his family home in north-east Victoria. But you just know that soon a committee will be formed to discuss building a national monument to him. And the police union will get the shits, yet again, and say that he was an outlaw and a criminal, but no one will listen to them much, and there will be some celebrity dickhead millionaire who will start it off with a whopping great donation, and then there'll be online campaigns and ads on Corn Flakes packets or something to donate for the Ned Kelly memorial, and they'll build something really inappropriate, like a giant abstract statue in Melbourne in the middle of Federation Square, that someone will climb up and fall off and die from the first week it is built, and then there'll be all this finger pointing and they'll take the statue and move it up to some empty pasture near the Hume Highway turn-off to Glenrowan where Japanese tourist buses will stop and all stand in front of it and take selfies making the peace-symbol salute around their heads, that probably means something else in Japan, and then drive off, wondering what the fuckishito that statue was all about.

Moonlite's bones, however, were another story. He was buried in the Anglican part of Rookwood Cemetery in Sydney and remained there for 107 years, continuing to fade out of memory. Finally, a few dedicated souls took up his cause and had his remains exhumed and reburied in Gundagai Cemetery.

If you visit the cemetery, you'll find this large rock under a big gum tree at the top of the cemetery engraved with the words:

> Andrew George Scott
> Captain Moonlite
> Born Ireland 8-1-1845
> Died Sydney 20-1-1880

And then a quote from his own written requests for burial:

> As to a monumental stone, a rough unhewn rock would be most fit, one that skilled hands could have made into something better. It will be like those it marks as kindness and charity could have shaped us to better ends. – Andrew George Scott.

And then:

> Laid to final rest near his friends James Nesbitt and Augustus Wernicke who lie in unmarked graves close by.

If you turn back around though, towards the centre of the cemetery, you'll see a tall white plinth that is the resting place of Constable Bowen-Webb, which reads in part:

> who was mortally wounded when bravely performing his duty in an encounter with armed criminals near Wantabadgery on the 17th of November 1879.

You can choose which one to dwell over or place flowers on. Or even both, if you're still undecided.

- - - -

A STRANGE APPARITION—NED KELLY'S FIGHT AND CAPTURE.

"His head, chest and sides were all protected with heavy plates of quarter-inch iron. Many shots hit him, yet he always recovered himself, and tapping his breast laughed derisively, as he coolly returned their fire. It appeared as if he were a fiend with a charmed life."—*The Age report.*

And still so many questions left unanswered at the end

Was Moonlite actually more wrong or wronged? Was it his nature or his circumstances that bought him down?

There are no easy answers. He was such a complex person. He was kind and cruel and erratic and loving and treacherous and self-obsessed and brilliant and deluded and vain and obsessed with the truth, and he was a liar, and I can't even begin to figure out what his Myers-Briggs profile might have been. He was all of these.

He was Doctor Doom and he was the Joker and he was the Riddler, but he was a superhero to us boys.

Clearly, there were many Moonlites. Each had a different story to tell, and each story was as true and accurate and as contradictory as the others. But, to the authorities, there was only one Moonlite – the evil and violent and predatory one, in need of being removed from society as a lesson to all who might be tempted to follow in his footsteps. And the last fact of the story is that he was actually created by society itself, who transformed him from Andrew George Scott into Captain Moonlite!

So, knowing all this, do you wonder how could it be that so few people have heard of him? How did he go from such notoriety to slip from the pages of history? Right from the Wantabadgery siege in late 1879 up to and after his hanging in January 1880, his story had dominated the press all around the colony. At least until the sensational Kelly gang's last stand at Glenrowan in June of that year. Then that was all anybody wanted to hear about.

But we're not going to talk about the Kellys, right?

Picture Credits

Frontispiece: attributed to Charles Nettleton, Victoria Police Historical Collection.

p. 7: State Library of Victoria, *Australasian Sketcher*, 28 November 1879.

p. 11: NSW State Archives and Records, ID: IE301765 NRS 2138, No. 2170.

p. 22: John T. Collins, State Library of Victoria, 1671162: jc004671.

p 29: Graham Bennett: Charge Sheet (NSW State Archives and Records, ID: IE99927 NRS2138 - 2172); Thomas Williams: Charge Sheet (NSW State Archives and Records, ID: IE361453 NRS2138 - 2173); Thomas Rogan: Prison Record (NSW State Archives and Records, ID: IE302299 NRS2138 - 2171); Gus Wernicke: (State Library of Victoria, *Australasian Sketcher*, 22 November 1879) Moonlite: (State Library of Victoria, *Australasian Sketcher*, 22 November 1879, p. 136).

p. 36: State Library of Victoria, *Australasian Sketcher*, 22 November 1879, p. 136.

pp. 60-61: State Library of Victoria, *Australasian Sketcher*, 22 November 1879, p. 136.

pp. 74-75: State Library of Victoria, *Illustrated Australian News*, 28 November 1879 p. 177.

p. 92: NSW State Archives and Records, NRS 13240 [X945].

p. 94: *The Bulletin*, Issue 1, 1880.

p. 98: Photo: Craig Cormick.

p. 102: *Australasian Sketcher*, July 17, 1880.

ABOUT QUEER OZ FOLK

Queer Oz Folk publishes histories from the gay, lesbian, bisexual, transgender, intersex and/or queer experience in Australia. We publish works by established academics, independent scholars and community historians, as well as reprints of significant material from the past. Our publishing is complemented by a website promoting these histories (www.queerozfolk.com.au).

We welcome publishing proposals. If you are interested in submitting a proposal please check out the information for authors on our website https://interventions.org.au/forauthors. If you think your proposal fits our guidelines please follow the submission process outlined there. Please note we are not currently publishing poetry or fiction.

Interventions has no independent source of income and is committed to keeping prices accessible. By supporting us you will help us keep queer history thriving and accessible to all. If you would like to support radical publishing in Australia please consider supporting our Patreon. Visit patreon.com/interventions to donate a small amount each month and get some great rewards.

Website: https://queerozfolk.com.au

Contact us: info@interventions.org.au or use the contact form on the website.

ABOUT THIS BOOK

The Queer Oz Folk editor and production project manager for this book was Graham Willett.

This book was copy edited by Eris Harrison of Effective Editing and was designed and laid out by Viktoria Ivanova of Vik Designs. Viktoria is a communication designer in Melbourne. She is a book publishing fiend, runs Spark Publishing Inc (for art-centric left books) and also designs for Victorian Socialists. Simon Strong designed the cover. Various kinds of assistance came from Craig Cormick, Wayne Murdoch and the committee of Interventions/Queer Oz Folk.

The Crime of Not Knowing Your Crime: Ric Throssell Against ASIO
By Karen Throssell
With a contextual essay by Phil Deery

"Through entwined poetry and prose, Karen Throssell illuminates ASIO's persecution of her extraordinary family. In the post 9/11 era, too many Australians have forgotten what happened in the Cold War. That's why this story matters."

Jeff Sparrow, writer and broadcaster

My grandmother was one of Australia's greatest novelists, my grandfather won the Victoria Cross for gallantry and my father was hounded all his life as a spy.

This is a three generational story. It's about my life; it's about my father, Ric; it's about my grandparents, the writer Katharine Susannah Prichard and the war hero Hugo Throssell.

It's a study of the psychology of spies and those who obsess about them, a narrative of guilt and innocence told through poetry, prose and historical documents.

— MORE FROM INTERVENTIONS —

Passionate Friends
Mary Fullerton, Mabel Singleton and Miles Franklin
Sylvia Martin

'A fascinating portrait of friendship, love, desire, politics and art - and the blurry, shape-shifting lines between them. I relished this book, rich in scholarship and full of heart.'

Clare Wright, author of *The Forgotten Rebels of Eureka* and *You Daughters of Freedom*

Mary Fullerton (1868 - 1946) and Mabel Singleton (1877 - 1965) met in Melbourne as suffrage and peace activists in Vida Goldstein's Women's Political Association. They remained together for 35 years as loving friends, raising Mabel's son born in 1911. Through her literary friendship with Miles Franklin (1879 - 1954), Mary Fullerton's last two volumes of poetry were published in the 1940s.

Rescued from near destruction, a box of Mary's manuscripts eventually made its way to the Mitchell Library. It contained poems she never sent to Mabel. These poignant poems trace a love story that sheds light on how women of the early twentieth century may have understood their love for each other.

— MORE FROM INTERVENTIONS —

www.ingramcontent.com/pod-product-compliance
Lightning Source LLC
Chambersburg PA
CBHW072340300426
44109CB00044B/2224